Beginner's Guide to

Pottery

Graham W. Bagg

Newnes Technical Books

Newnes Technical Books

is an imprint of the Butterworth Group
which has principal offices in
London, Boston, Durban, Singapore, Sydney, Toronto, Wellington

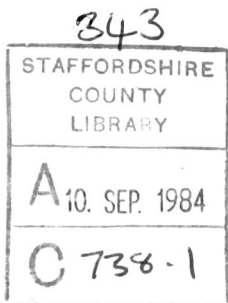

First published 1984

© Butterworth & Co (Publishers) Ltd, 1984

British Library Cataloguing in Publication Data

Bagg, Graham W.
  Beginner's guide to pottery.
  1. Pottery craft
  I. Title
  738.1   TT920

  ISBN 0-408-01436-9

Photoset by Butterworths Litho Preparation Department
Printed in England by Page Bros Ltd, Norwich, Norfolk

Preface

All true craftwork embodies two disciplines: on the one hand the development of special skills and manual dexterity, and on the other, the cultivation of an aesthetic awareness manifesting itself in a beauty of form which is complemented by a measure of apt and restrained embellishment. Few crafts illustrate this dichotomy better than pottery where the balance between one aspect and the other fluctuates between a bias towards pure art, as in china painting, and the almost pure craft displayed in the making of a plaster mould.

Techniques of making and decorating are numerous and can be applied at every stage of production. It is good for the student to experience as many of these as possible but a preference for, and specialisation in, one or more styles will, in most cases, inevitably follow.

Pottery, like any form of craftwork, can only be fully appreciated by one who has personal experience of its practice, its many problems and the diverse skills involved. It is therefore gratifying to find more schools providing instruction in ceramics and more and more adults anxious to experience the excitement of working in clay. Most local authorities provide tuition at evening classes and adult centres and at some of these, extended weekend and vacation courses are arranged to give the student a chance to study the craft in more depth. Craft skills are best acquired through personal instruction and by watching practical demonstrations by a competent craftsman.

This, however, is useless without regular practice over an extended period. Ideal conditions for a beginner are the provision of home facilities for regular practice and experimentation, coupled with a course at a weekly evening class to enable contact to be made with an experienced potter, to witness demonstrations of method, and to become familiar with a variety of techniques.

For those out of reach of an evening class but who are able to set up a modest home pottery, a good, well-illustrated pottery manual must take the place of personal tuition. Instructional film strips and slides, together with relevant cassette commentaries which demonstrate all aspects and techniques of the craft, and which also provide illustrated examples of the work of well-known potters, are available from firms supplying materials to craft potters.

Finally, careful examination of pottery produced in past generations, as can be seen in our major museums, together with that being produced by contemporary potters, is invaluable both to observe how the many techniques have been exploited and to provide inspiration. Indeed, an unconscious assessment of every pot seen or handled is the mark of an enthusiastic potter.

I wish to thank my son, Simon, for his invaluable help in the checking of the manuscript.

G.W.B.

Contents

1

Setting up a home pottery

Pottery is not an activity to be carried out in the living room of the average house. Clay can be both wet and dusty and walls may be splashed and ledges lined with dust. Glaze ingredients, too, are dusty and in some cases toxic and must never be used in an area where food is stored or eaten. During firing the kiln creates a hot, fumy atmosphere and the need for repeated clearing away of work soon becomes frustrating.

The siting of a pottery must largely depend upon the layout of the home premises. In a country home or farmstead it might be possible to adapt an outhouse or vacant garage for the purpose. For those with more limited space available a shed erected in the garden will probably provide the best solution. Ideally a pottery should have a concrete or tiled floor to make a solid base for the wheel and work table and to facilitate cleaning. If the kiln can be housed in a separate area so much the better, but if it must be sited in the same shed, ventilation should be provided immediately above it. A wooden roof should be shielded from heat by a local lining of 'Formica' or a similar type of laminate.

A pottery room will need to be electrically wired to provide lighting and power for the wheel and kiln. If three-phase power is available this will reduce the running costs of the kiln. To have water on tap is also desirable. Failing this, water for the wheel and the washing of hands and utensils can be carried out from the house in a few large buckets before each session.

If you do have piped water, bear in mind that the regular washing of clay-covered hands, tools and utensils in a sink can cause serious silting-up of the plumbing. Clay washing is best carried out in a bucket of water, where the clay solid can be allowed to settle and disposed of separately from the water.

Equipment

The essential items of equipment are outlined below.
Furniture
A firm table at which to work, preferably covered with a plastic laminate top for ease of cleaning.
A wedging slab for preparation of the clay. This can take the form of a small, rigidly made bench or table. The legs must be supported by a stout underframe, since the slab will need to remain firm as heavy lumps of clay are thrown upon it. A springy table will dissipate much of the energy put into the act of wedging. The table top can be of stout close-grained

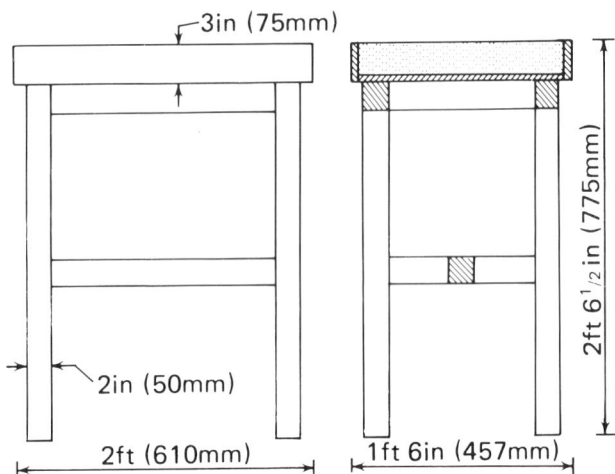

Figure 1.1. Construction of a wedging slab with suggested sizes

hardwood or thinner wood, lipped with a surround to form a 2 inch (50 mm) well in which cement or plaster can be cast and levelled (Figure 1.1).

A wedging surface must not be too porous or smooth to prevent the clay from adhering to it and must not be too high or wedging will become tiring – 30 inches (762 mm) is a good height. The making of such a wedging table should be well within the capabilities of the average amateur wood-worker but if a specific slab cannot be provided, wedging will have to be carried out on a plaster or cement slab positioned over the leg of the ordinary work table. Remember to clear the work table first since the vibration caused by wedging will be considerable.

A damp box
A damp box is necessary to store unfinished work pending later completion. This is one of the most essential items of equipment. A very cheap and efficient damp box can be made from an old galvanised iron domestic water tank. Such tanks are readily available from local plumbing and heating contractors. Any holes can be sealed by placing a large

Figure 1.2. Method for sealing pipe holes in a dismantled galvanised iron water tank

washer on either side and pressing them together with a bolt and nut of suitable length and gauge. The joint can, if necessary, be made watertight with a little sealer (Figure 1.2).

A fairly thick layer of cement is then cast onto the inside base which can be kept regularly damp. A lid can be constructed to cover the opening or it can simply be covered with a sheet of stout polythene. In a tank of this sort, leather-hard pots will keep workable for weeks. Pots should be placed on a support, such as an upturned plastic flower pot, to prevent the clay bases from taking up water and disintegrating.

Small items can be kept damp in the simple type of seed propagating case which is available from seed merchants and garden centres. If none of these facilities can be provided, pots can always be prevented from further drying by sealing them in plastic bags.

Shelving
Shelving will be necessary for the storage of materials and some slatted shelves will be required for the storage of pots during drying.

Hardware
Plastic clay is delivered in sealed polythene but when the seal is broken, it is liable to dry out and become too hard to be worked. Once the bag has been opened, it is wise to store the clay in a plastic container. *Plastic dustbins* with lids are best. The clay should be sealed in with a polythene sheet before the lid is replaced.

Household *plastic buckets* and *bowls* are invaluable for the storage and preparation of clay slips and glazes and as receptacles for slop clay and turnings.

A *beam, spring,* or *counter balance* for the weighing of plaster, glaze ingredients, and balls of clay.

When the student progresses to the weighing out of glaze recipes, many of the colouring oxides will need to be added in only small quantities; these will prove difficult to weigh on the ordinary balance. A *chemical balance* is a luxury but the 'Fulham'-type balance scale weighing a maximum of 125 g is inexpensive and will meet the need satisfactorily (Figure 1.3).

An *aluminium or styrene jug* of 1 litre (approx. 2 pints) capacity, graduated in fluid ozs and millilitres.

Large plastic containers with screw-on tops are discarded after emptying by sweet shops and the proprietor is usually willing, if asked, for these to be collected. Fishmongers, too, often retail stout plastic containers in which shellfish have

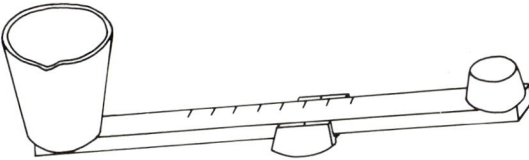

Figure 1.3. A simple beam balance useful for weighing small quantities of chemicals

been received. Both these types of container are suitable for storing ready-mixed glaze, since the large tops allow for easy stirring. Screw-top glass coffee jars can be useful for storing smaller quantities of glaze and dry materials, such as metallic oxide powders.

Kiln and wheel

The tools required for pottery are relatively few in number, much of the work being done by the hands alone or with the aid of small items which come readily to hand, but there are two items requiring much greater expenditure – the kiln and a potter's wheel. Of the two, the kiln is the more important and if an initial choice has to be made this must constitute the first priority. Much pottery can be made without a wheel but none can be properly finished without a kiln. A wheel can always be added to the equipment as and when the budget permits. The choice of kiln and wheel is discussed as they are introduced (see pages 20 and 148).

Smaller items of equipment

Bleached natural sponges, one of medium texture, and two small sponges of fine texture, one of which should be wired or bound to a 12 inch (300 mm) length of thin bamboo cane for use as a sponge stick. This is used when throwing, to soak up surplus water from the inside of a tall or very narrow-mouthed pot.

A few boxwood modelling tools, the various patterns of which are quoted in a catalogue by code letters or numbers. Those with rounded and slightly cranked working surfaces, usually described as spatula tools, will prove to be the most versatile.

5

A 4 or 5 inch (100 or 125 mm) *palette knife* for grinding
colours and a few small panes of glass on which the colours
can be ground. Also a 120 mesh *sieve* (lawn) together with a
1 inch (25 mm) pure bristle *lawn brush*, and a pair of 8 inch
(200 mm) *callipers* are useful.

Brushes for decorating, as required. Much can be achieved
with a few squirrel pencils of various sizes and a flat duster
type will prove of value for laying on large areas of slip.

A set of turning tools. A useful turning tool can be made by
bending a piece of old clock spring to form a hoop and
screwing or binding it tightly with a fine cord to the sides of a
hardwood handle (Figure 1.4).

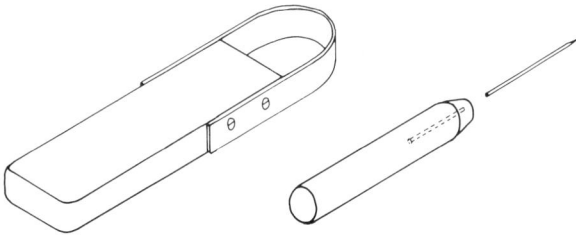

Figure 1.4. A home-made hoop turning tool and pricker

A *pestle and mortar* can be most useful but is not an
essential item of equipment for a beginner and can always be
added at a later date.

All the following tools can also be purchased but are not
difficult to make at home:

A *clay wire cutter* which can be assembled by cutting or
filing a small groove around the centre of two 3 inch (75 mm)
lengths of ½ inch (12 mm) dowel rod, into which the two
ends of a length of 24 gauge stainless steel wire are fixed. A
4 oz (100 g) coil of this wire will last a potter for a long while
and should always be on hand in case of breakages.

A *needle* for use on the wheel can be made by filing the
pointed end of a 2–2½ inch (50–65 mm) wire nail to an even
taper, then cutting off the flat head and gluing this cut end
with a spot of quick setting epoxy resin glue (such as

'Araldite') into a fine hole drilled into the end of a 3 inch (75 mm) piece of ½ inch (12 mm) dowel. A simpler, but less permanent alternative can be made by sticking a hat pin through a cork.

A *side cutter* for use on the wheel can be made by bending a piece of mild steel and filing the cutting edges to

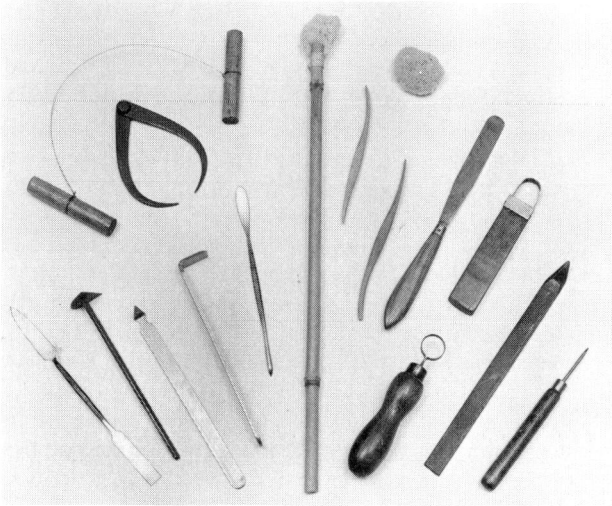

Figure 1.5. A selection of essential pottery tools. *Left of central sponge stick* (back row): twisted wire cutter and callipers; (front row): three types of turning tool and two patterns of steel modelling tool. *Right of central sponge stick* (back row): two boxwood modelling tools, sponge, palette knife and hoop tool; (front row): coiler, side tool and pricker

shape. *Modelling boards* can be cut from ½ inch (12 mm) waterproof ply or block-board and *wooden slats* to control thickness when rolling out clay can be obtained from any DIY shop. *A wooden roller* about 2 inch (50 mm) in diameter (Figure 1.5) can be bought or made. Finally, many uses will be found for old kitchen and pocket *knives*.

2

The process of pottery making

Before launching into a detailed study of the techniques of pottery making, it would seem wise to present a short outline of the main phases through which clay must pass in order to emerge as an attractive and usable article.

A pot must first of all be fashioned to give it a basic form, either by throwing on a potter's wheel, by making a casting from a plaster of Paris mould, or by employing one of the hand-building methods described in Chapter 8. The pot is then dried until it becomes sufficiently stiff to handle safely but still damp enough for further work to be carried out. It is during this stage that most thrown pots will be turned using the potter's wheel as a vertical lathe, to create tidy feet and fitted lids. At this stage any individual clay components such as handles and spouts are assembled and added.

When the pot is fully made, time must be allowed for a thorough drying of the clay. The dried pot is then packed into the kiln and subjected to its first baking during which those physical and chemical changes in the clay take place which bring about the qualities of hardness and strength normally associated with pottery. After this the pot will have shrunk appreciably in size and, at least in the case of earthenware, still be porous. To render the newly-baked pot impervious to water, it is covered with powdered glaze, suspended in water, then repacked in the kiln and given a second firing with the object of fusing the glaze onto the surface in the form of a glassy layer.

It should be noted that decoration can be added at any, or all, of the stages outlined.

Once-fired ware (green-glazed ware)

Some potters by-pass the first firing by coating the dry clay pot with the glaze and maturing both clay and glaze in one and the same operation. This, of course, will save firing costs but it is not a suitable method for beginners, and the rate of failure can be high. Fully dried-out clay presents the pot in its most brittle and vulnerable form and to handle it at this stage is fraught with danger. Some potters seek to compromise by glazing before the clay has fully dried, but this can cause the glaze to run due to the diminished porosity. Dry clay will absorb moisture from the water-based glaze which will inevitably tend to soften it. This can be particularly dangerous when dealing with small handles which are relatively thin in cross-section, but possess a large surface area. Predamping of these parts is sometimes practised to obviate the problem. An interval is often allowed to elapse between glazing the inside and outside surfaces in an attempt to limit total-water absorption at any one time.

Another problem inherent in the once-fired technique is the very real danger of glaze bubbling caused by an escape of volatile gases from the clay body which would normally have been lost during the initial firing.

3

The origin and nature of clays

The craft of pottery is based on the raw material of clay and it is therefore advantageous for a beginner who seriously intends to master the techniques of the craft to learn something about the nature and properties of this material. Many of the processes involved are of a chemical nature and formulae, the chemist's shorthand, are included throughout. However this should not deter the non-scientist from understanding the basic principles.

Origins

Clays are derived from minerals collectively known as *feldspars* which are themselves constituents of primary rock such as granite. The feldspars are made up of three basic components: silica, as flint, quartz or sand (SiO_2); alumina (Al_2O_3); and an alkali such as potash or soda. As a result of hydrothermal processes in which acid solutions move upwards, the feldspars disintegrate into three separate substances. The potash or soda combines with the carbon dioxide to form pearl ash (K_2CO_3) or soda ash (Na_2CO_3), both of which being soluble go into solution in the surrounding soil. The alumina combines with some of the silica and water to form hydrous aluminium silicate which is, quite simply, clay. Some free silica remains as quartz and quantities of micaceous materials present in the parent rock are freed.

$$\overset{Na_2}{K_2OAl_2O_36SiO_2} \; + \; \underbrace{H_2O+CO_2}_{H_2CO_3} \; \rightarrow \; \overset{Na_2}{K_2CO_3+4SiO_2}$$

$$+ \; \boxed{Al_2O_32SiO_22H_2O}$$

CLAY

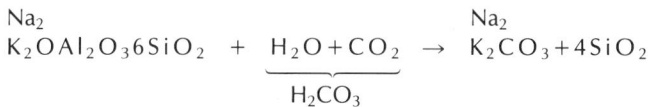

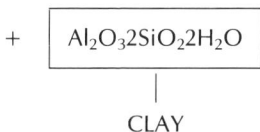

The two chemical components of clay, silica and alumina, are laid down as layers and it is the movement of one layer upon another which allows clay to be plastic and malleable.

Primary clay

This is clay which has remained *in situ*, a typical example being the Cornish china clay deposits. It cannot be dug and is obtained by the action of high-pressure hoses on the clay face. The resultant slurry is led off into settling troughs where any quartz and micaceous material is separated out. Huge conical-shaped tips of these materials, together with the overburden from the past, still dot the mining areas such as St. Austell, but since the 1966 Aberfan disaster, the sand, overburden and other wastes have to be sorted into separate plateau-shaped heaps.

Secondary clay

In many instances, clay is formed in the catchment areas of streams and rivers and over many thousands of years gradually is eroded and carried along by the water. As streams reach lower levels they run more sluggishly and in many cases flow over natural depressions in the earth allowing the clay particles, carried in suspension, to be deposited, perhaps hundreds of miles from their point of origin. Over many years, deposits build-up until a bed of clay is laid down.

This is known as secondary clay and is recovered for use by digging. The 'Ball clays' of Dorset and Devon are secondary clays. (These are so-called because in the 19th century they were transported in 35 pound balls.) In the journey from their point of origin, secondary clays accumulate impurities. Devon and Dorsetshire clays are grey or blue in colour due to the presence of carbonaceous impurities. These burn away in the kiln to leave a cream colour. Some pick up iron oxides and so appear yellow or brown and usually fire to a terracotta.

In addition, all secondary clays gather impurities in the form of metallic oxides, such as soda ash, potash, lime or magnesia and some contain a proportion of illite derived from the mica. Most secondary clays therefore contain all the ingredients necessary for the making of a glaze (see Chapter 11). Indeed some of these clays can be applied as a slip glaze over a clay with a higher maturing point. *Fireclay* is a different type of secondary clay and, due to earth upheavals, is now found deep in the earth, often between coal seams. As its name implies, it is very refractory.

Primary clay, having remained *in situ*, has had no opportunity to incorporate impurities and is therefore 98 per cent pure, but it is large-particled and therefore not very plastic so that it is not suitable for use on a potter's wheel. It contains no oxides of metals (fluxes) and, owing to its purity, it is perfectly white. The absence of fluxes means that it will be possible to subject it to great heat without the occurrence of fusion, in other words, it will be very refractory and will remain white when fired. Secondary clay, on the other hand, has been subjected to continual grinding by the action of water, and is consequently composed of very fine particles. It has also become allied with a number of metallic fluxes. This means that ball clay will throw well but will have a relatively low fusibility. Its fine texture will also tend to make it sticky and non-porous.

A usable clay must satisfy three main requirements: it must be plastic enough to mould; suitably open to prevent cracking during drying; and sufficiently fusible to allow varying degrees of vitrification, in other words, to possess the required density and refractory quality. To obtain all the optimum qualities in one clay, the potter blends them in varying proportions, adding other beneficial materials which may be lacking. Such blends are known as *bodies* and their composition is varied to suit the use for which they are intended.

Table 3.1 summarises the qualities which have been discussed. Recipes for clay bodies are as numerous as glaze recipes, but it is hoped that the examples given will illustrate how the principle of blending to achieve fitness for purpose is applied. Earthenware will need to be sufficiently plastic to throw, will need to have enough refractory material added to allow a satisfactory firing to 1100°C, and enough flint to maintain an open texture. Stoneware will need to fire to a slightly higher temperature and to be more fusible, yet at the same time remain throwable. Porcelain will probably be cast so little plasticity is called for, but the blend will need to be kept open, strong and above all be vitreous at high temperatures, so ample fluxing material must be added in the form of feldspar.

The beginner is advised to commence by purchasing ready-made bodies, taking note particularly of the recommended firing temperatures and matching them with the firing range of the available kiln. If a full temperature range is possible it is good to have a supply of a red earthenware body, a smaller quantity of a contrasting white earthenware for the making of slipwares, and a buff body usable as either earthenware or stoneware. It should be abundantly clear by now that it is not satisfactory to dig some local clay and expect immediate success. Even if it were an ideal clay it would need arduous and time-consuming preparation and well over a year of weathering before it could be used.

The firing process

Even pots which appear to be thoroughly dry still contain quite a lot of free water. During firing this will gradually turn to steam as the temperature of the kiln rises above the

Table 3.1 Components of a body

Type of body	Qualities					Examples of body composition		
	Plasticity	Porosity	Density/fusibility	Refractive quality	Whiteness	Earthenware	Stoneware	Porcelain
China clay				✓	✓	30%	30%	50%
Ball clay	✓		✓			40%	30%	
Flint		✓		✓		10%	8%	25%
Cornish stone (china stone)			✓			20%	30%	
Fire clay		✓		✓				
Feldspar			✓				2%	25%

boiling point of water (100°C). As has already been seen, clay is made up of one part alumina, 2 parts silica and 2 parts of chemically-combined water. As the temperature climbs above 350°C, this chemically-combined water will begin to leave the clay, vacating spaces into which the remaining clay contracts. Above 1000°C glassy material will begin to form as the alumina, silica and flux in the body begin to behave as a glaze. This is the process known as *vitrification* and it is this which imparts density to the biscuit. The extent of vitrification will vary from one type of ware to another and is largely responsible for the broad classification of wares which is generally adopted.

Types of pottery

The preceding study of clay bodies and the nature of the changes brought about by firing have a direct bearing on the characteristics associated with the three acknowledged types of pottery. Much of the distinction between them is based on the degree of vitrification attained.

Earthenware is rarely fired above 1150°C, so little glassy material forms to fill the pores of the clay. As a result, earthenware is always porous when biscuited and fairly soft. This is an ideal quality for a flower-pot but any domestic earthenware must be covered with a non-porous glaze to render it waterproof.

Stoneware has a firing range between 1200°C and 1300°C at which temperature the clay becomes partially vitrified so making a much denser article. Stoneware is consequently impermeable and a well-fired stoneware pot will be watertight even without a glaze. Some bodies can either be fired to 1100°C to produce earthenware, or fired to the higher temperature of 1230°C to form stoneware.

Earthenware and stoneware are opaque. The one feature which distinguishes *porcelain* is its translucency. With its high proportion of refractory china clay and flint and the fluxing feldspar, porcelain can be fired up to 1350°C and often above. Vitrification is pushed to its limits and the body virtually becomes a non-deforming opaque glaze, thus exhibiting a translucent quality. True porcelain body is essentially non-plastic and various recipes have been compounded to rectify this, usually by adding a percentage of ball clay or the very plastic Bentonite. Although these additions allow the body to be thrown, they tend to mar its essential quality. English bone china is a rather softer form of porcelain, firing at a stoneware temperature. It contains a high proportion of bone ash to act as flux which renders it translucent.

Shrinkage

When designing pieces of pottery, note must be taken of the shrinkage which occurs during firing. A teacup, for example, which appears after making to be of standard size, will be far too small when it emerges from the kiln. Stoneware and earthenware can be expected to shrink by one tenth and porcelain by one sixth to one eighth of its original size.

Clay states

The potter uses clay in many forms. If plastic clay is shredded into small pieces and churned with water, it forms a slurry which, after sieving through an 80s lawn, constitutes *clay slip*. In this form, clay can be used as a cement and is essential for many decorative techniques. In its *plastic* form, clay is suitable for throwing and hand modelling. When it has become partially dry and is capable of being handled without fear of distortion, it is said to be *leather-hard* and in this form can be turned, carved, cut, and portions of it luted together. Before being kilned, clay must have dried out completely. In this state, it is at its most vulnerable and, being extremely brittle, must be handled with great care.

Lean or *short* is a term often applied to a clay which is lacking in plasticity. At the opposite end of the scale, a highly plastic clay is described as being *fat*.

Preparing clay for use

Plastic clay, as received from the suppliers, is not necessarily ready for immediate use as it may contain trapped pockets of air. These might cause problems when throwing but, more seriously, the air would expand during subsequent firing causing severe blow-outs in the biscuit. Not only will the individual pot suffer but damage can be inflicted on other articles in the kiln. If you cut the lump of clay with a wire any pockets of air will be readily visible. The air can be removed by the related techniques of wedging and kneading.

Wedging and kneading

The top of a lump of clay is first patted into a dome shape using the cupped palms of both hands. The mass is then cut horizontally into two with a clay-cutting wire and the top portion picked up in both hands, inverted and banged down

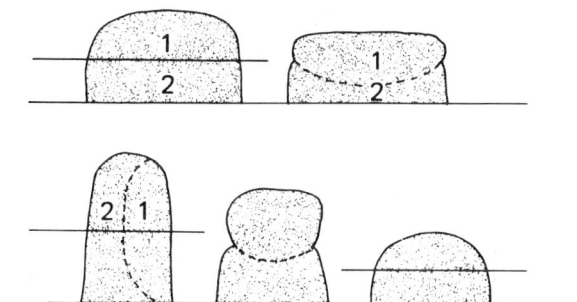

Figure 3.1. Wedging

vigorously onto the remaining clay. The dome bursts any air bubbles within its range. The lump of clay is then peeled from the wedging slab, turned up on end and the whole process repeated. The word 'peeled' is used advisedly since any attempt to lift the clay by pressing the fingers against it at the point where it rests on the slab inevitably leads to the two adhering to each other. The same sequence is continued until the wire reveals a bubble-free surface. Continual turning of the clay not only exposes the maximum volume to the wedging action but ensures that the clay remains in a manageable lump (Figure 3.1).

Wedging is followed by kneading. With the mass of clay on the wedging slab, pull the back portion forward with the fingers and bring it towards you, then push it away again forcibly with the heel of both hands (Figure 3.2). The

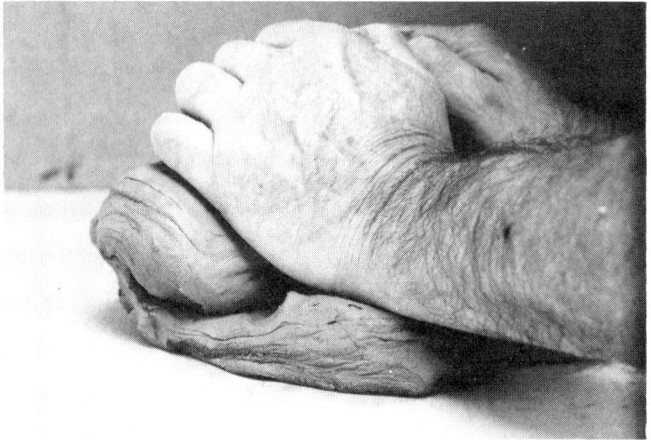

Figure 3.2. Kneading

technique is similar to that used for knocking air out of bread dough. As in wedging, the clay is given a quarter turn before the action is repeated and the procedure continued until the clay feels perfectly even. One final cut with the wire will confirm that no air bubbles remain.

Maintaining a workable condition

Work on the wheel will inevitably result in the production of much wet, sloppy clay and subsequent turning will yield dry shreds of leather-hard clay. It is a good plan to keep both in the same container where they will tend to balance one

18

another out and can later be kneaded and wedged back to a usable plastic state. If the resultant mixture is still far too sticky, it can be spread out to dry on a flat surface, preferably of plaster of Paris, which, being very porous, will absorb much of the surplus moisture. This is a somewhat tedious, but very necessary, process. If a batch of clay has become too hard for throwing on the wheel, very wet clay can be spread between layers of it prior to kneading. Ideally, wet and dry clay is recycled by using a pug mill which mechanically churns and extrudes a plastic mixture. Pug mills however are expensive and not really justifiable in an amateur pottery.

Grog

Grog is fired biscuit which has been reground. It is incorporated into bodies to keep them more open and so reduce warping and shrinkage. It is available in several grades and can be introduced into clay during the wedging procedure by sprinkling it on each cut layer, complete mixing being accomplished by the final kneading.

4

Work on the potter's wheel

Many would-be potters have first been attracted to the craft by watching a pot rapidly grow from a mere lump of clay in the hands of an experienced thrower. The process of throwing is a very personal and spontaneous one and perhaps more than any other activity distinguishes the individual work of the studio potter from the more mechanically produced ware of his industrial counterpart. It is a skill which can only be acquired by regular practice and experience and by a readiness to learn from mistakes. It demands, in the initial stages, no little amount of determination and will to succeed, together with a willingness to discard unsuccessful attempts. Too many ash trays have been made from failed jugs or bowls.

Choosing a wheel

There are two basic types of potter's wheel, the kick wheel and the power-driven wheel. When setting up a modest home pottery there may well be some difficulty in making a wise choice. From the beginner's point of view, there is little doubt that the former type will complicate early attempts at throwing by the extra co-ordination required for the kicking action. Many kick wheels are fitted with fly-wheels which are too light to maintain sufficient momentum to allow a kick-free performance during more delicate operations or to provide the necessary assistance when centring a large lump of clay. Geared kick wheels have been introduced in an attempt to improve performance and to make the action less tiring.

A power wheel will inevitably cost more but has infinitely more to offer the serious potter. There are many power wheels on the market from which to choose and the choice is largely a personal one. If at all possible, it is wise to try a selection first-hand at a potter's shop or warehouse to discover which feels right and comfortable to use – leg length and height can be the deciding factors. The mechanisms which make possible variations in the speed of rotation vary from one wheel to another. Some feature a friction drive in which a small leather-covered friction wheel moves across the diameter of the flywheel, others rely on the double-cone principle, some modify this traditional cone-drive into one incorporating a cone and ring, and others embody purely electrical devices such as transformers or thyristors. Whatever the action it is advisable to choose a wheel which will cater for a low bottom speed without loss of torque so useful when finishing taller pots. All will give the higher speed ratio necessary for centring. Rigidity is another important factor to consider and it would be wise to purchase a wheel capable of handling a maximum of 10 lb (5 kg) clay.

Throwing

An examination of a random group of thrown pots will reveal that the vast majority are built-up from three basic units: the cylinder, which can be modified into convex or concave profiles; the bowl, in its many forms; and the shape characteristic of a bottle top. It is therefore essential for a student to become proficient in the throwing of these important shapes.

Throwing a cylinder
Cut a piece of clay with the wire from a lump which has been throughly wedged – about 2 lb (916 g) is a good size for a first

exercise. Pat it with cupped hands to form a rough ball. Moisten the wheelhead with a sponge which has been wetted and then well squeezed. A wet wheel will prevent the clay from adhering to it. Now throw the ball of clay smartly onto the centre of the wheel so that it is held firmly in place. If the aim has been poor, the clay can be corrected by wrapping the fingers around the ball and pulling it to the centre. The amount of effort required will be considerable and gives some indication of the degree of adhesion between the clay and the wheel.

It is extremely important to adopt a good position at the wheel, standing or sitting well up to it and crouching over the clay. Now set the wheel in motion (anti-clockwise); the irregularities and eccentricity of the ball of clay will be very apparent. The first task in throwing is to iron out these irregularities and to manipulate the clay so that it is running perfectly true on the wheel. This process is known as centring and is assisted by a reasonable wheel speed. Both hands and the clay should be well lubricated with water and the hands wrapped around the ball so that the fingers overlap, the little fingers should run on the wheel and the palms be positioned diametrically opposite one another. The arms should be well supported against the body and the elbows well back, to give stability to the hands; long arms make for added leverage.

Pressure is now brought to bear on the clay by squeezing the palms together and at the same time gradually raising them upwards. The irregularities will still be apparent but sustained pressure will begin to smooth out the bumps and to lift them upwards so that the clay will assume a very irregular top surface. To avoid this, a process known as coning is adopted. Instead of maintaining a fixed hand position, overlap the fingers as they are brought up the side of the clay, so that the opening between the palms is gradually reduced forcing the clay to form an inverted-cone shape. Since this is pointed, the irregularities disappear. It must be remembered that the diameter will become smaller and smaller as the cone is formed so that hand pressure must be varied accordingly (Figure 4.1).

Figure 4.1. Basic throwing movements. Top left: coning. Top right: depressing. Above left: the first opening of the clay mass. Above right: the second opening of the clay mass

Throughout this, and every other throwing activity, the clay and hands must be regularly moistened with water. Upward movement of the hands forming the cone can be followed by a corresponding downward one in which the fingers operate in the reverse manner. There is no need for the hands to leave the clay; keep them moving in both directions until a satisfactory cone is created. A pot cannot be made from a slender cone-shape so the clay must now be brought back to a usable dome-shaped mass on the wheel. This is achieved by a movement known as *depressing*. The left hand is bent at the knuckles to form a right-angle and the thumb braced against the side of the first finger as far back towards the wrist as possible. Assuming this position will create a pad at the base of the thumb which is brought to rest on the apex of the cone, the fingers being positioned obliquely down its side. Holding the hand in this position, press downwards. The top of the cone will begin to grow into a mushroom-shape. Continued pressure with this one hand would eventually swell the shape and make it unmanageable. To prevent this take the right hand in a similar position placing the fingers on those of the left hand with the right thumb resting on the left. The role of the right hand is to exert continual pressure on the side of the 'mushroom' formed as the clay is forced downwards by the left hand to resolve it into the main mass. Provided the hands are maintained in their respective positions the clay will assume a workable shape on the wheel. The temptation to open the right-angle formed by the left hand must be resisted until the finger tips reach the surface of the wheel when both hands can be gradually moved over to the position adopted at the beginning of the centring process.

If the clay still feels eccentric, coning and depressing must be repeated until it is running perfectly true. It is useless to proceed further until centring has been accomplished. Continued practice will speed up the operation and coning and depressing will become one continuous movement.

Once the clay is running perfectly true, the wheel speed should be decreased and *hollowing* can begin. Rest the hands once again around opposing sides of the clay and whilst maintaining this position locate its centre with the thumb of the left hand. When this has been found, the thumb is slowly fed down into the clay until it is about ½ inch (12 mm) from the level of the wheel, the fingers acting as a guide fence.

The initial opening must now be widened until it assumes the same internal base diameter as that of the proposed cylinder. This second opening of the mass is brought about by gripping the left wrist with the right finger tips and leaning well over to allow the right thumb to reach inside the initial opening until its tip just reaches the base. Now press the pad at the tip of the thumb outwards directly towards you until the desired size is obtained. The outer wall is supported by the fingers of the left hand which are wrapped around it.

At all stages of throwing, pressure from one hand must always be matched by supporting pressure from the other. At the end of this movement both hands are moved gently upwards and the clay is allowed to slide gracefully from them. This focuses attention on another important principle: a throwing movement should always be fully completed and the hands never snatched from the clay at any intermediate stage.

The embryo pot will now have an inside and an outside but the walls will be both thick and short and the inside corners very concave. These corners can be squared with the aid of a piece of square-ended slate or close-grained timber held vertically on the inside base of the clay with the finger tips of both hands to the front and both thumbs to the back. As the wheel revolves, the slate is gradually moved across the base to the right until the convex corner is pressed into a right-angle (Figure 4.2).

Height is imparted to the cylinder by raising the clay contained in the thick wall upwards without allowing any increase in its diameter. This will, at the same time, reduce the wall to an acceptable thickness. Lifting the wall is perhaps the most difficult aspect of throwing for the beginner, requiring considerable control and confidence which can only come through repeated practice. The primary aim should be to adopt correct habits from the beginning, remembering that clay can only be thrown by squeezing it between two opposing pressures; it does not stretch. To lift the wall, bend the first finger of the right hand at the second knuckle and tuck the remaining fingers away tightly into the palm. The thumb should be pushed away as far as possible from the bent finger and the whole hand arched to enable both wheel and clay to be touched by the thumb and the bent knuckle. In this position the side of the bent finger can sit vertically against the outer clay wall. Place the fingers of the left hand against the inside of the pot to oppose the outward position of the right. Now move both hands

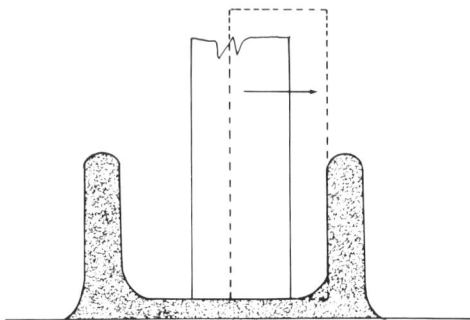

Figure 4.2. Using the slate to square the inside corners of the pot

together up the sides of the clay. To ensure that the hands work in unison, the student is advised to allow the left hand thumb to hang over the rim of the clay and to let it rest on the back of the right hand. When sufficiently confident, press the knuckle of the right hand into the clay at wheel level to create a small groove and then move both hands slowly up the clay wall, applying pressure simultaneously between the crooked finger of the right hand and the middle finger of the left hand. Support is provided either side by the remaining fingers (Figure 4.3).

If the lift has been well carried out, the original groove made at the clay base will have been maintained until it is finally lost at the rim. Pressure must be relaxed as the top is reached and the clay allowed, as before, to slip away through the fingers. A continual watch is necessary to maintain an even diameter. Uneven pressure between the hands will lead to distortion of the cylindrical shape and sudden variations in pressure will produce walls which are thicker on one side than on the other and result in 'pot wobble'. It will be necessary to make several lifts in order to obtain the correct height and wall thickness and it is advisable to keep the top a little thicker (*at first*) and to thin this progressively by subsequent raising.

Figure 4.3. Lifting the clay wall

Should the top of the pot become uneven it can be levelled with the pricker. Hold the tip of the first finger and the thumb of the left hand freely over the rim of the clay. Allow the needle to rest across the thumb with its point facing in the direction of rotation of the wheel and gradually feed it through the clay until it meets the inside finger tip. At this

Figure 4.4. Levelling the top of a pot with the pricker

point, the surplus clay is detached and can be lifted away (Figure 4.4).

The natural shape of the knuckle will create a concave shape at the point where the outside wall meets the wheel. This can be trimmed square using a side tool (Figure 4.5), cutting down vertically with the left-hand edge of the tool, then pivoting it on the wheel to bring the right-hand edge into play to clear the clay from the wheel-head.

Repeated attempts should be made to throw an even cylinder and it is a wise plan to cut a practice cylinder vertically in half to examine its cross section.

Shaping the cylinder

A shaped pot is created by assuming the same lifting procedure but applying uneven pressures between the left and right hands. If the inner pressure is applied slightly above the outer, a concave shape will result and if the outer pressur is exerted above the inner, the profile will become convex. By varying these pressures, it is possible to develop compound curves. The chosen shape affects the basic cylinder: widening results in loss of height and thinning of the wall whereas narrowing will have the opposite effect. Therefore if a pot with a very convex profile is planned, the wall of the initial clay cylinder must be left considerably thicker.

On completion, any water left inside should be mopped out with the sponge stick. To remove the pot from the wheel,

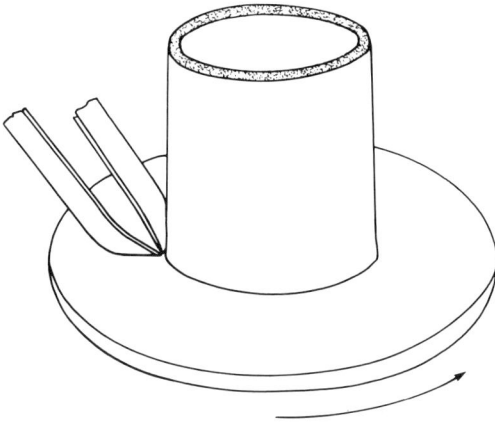

Figure 4.5. Using the side tool to clean up the pot base prior to cutting it free, as seen from the back of the wheel

flood the wheel with water and hold a wire, flat and very taut on the wheel. Push this smartly underneath the base of the pot. The wire carries the water with it and so breaks the suction. It is wise to repeat the action a second time. After this the pot can be slid onto the open left hand by pressing the right hand finger tips lightly against its base. Alternatively lift the pot off directly with the fingers and thumbs of both hands. Transfer to a waiting board to harden (Figure 4.6). Removing the pot is a somewhat daunting experience for a beginner but none-the-less needs to be done quickly and confidently.

Throwing a bowl

Unlike a flat dish, the inside of a bowl should display a perfect curve and this must be remembered throughout its making. Once the line of the curve has been lost it is practically impossible to rstore it. The ball of clay is centred in exactly the same manner as for the cylinder and the initial

Figure 4.6. Using the wire to cut the pot free from the wheel

opening made with the thumb. A flat inside base is, however, not required, so the subsequent widening movement must be modified. The hands are arranged exactly as for widening the cylinder base, but when throwing the bowl the pressure exerted by the thumb is not merely directed outwards but also progressively upwards in unison with the supporting left hand. The natural curve of the thumb tip will produce a clean curve in the clay (Figure 4.7).

Figure 4.7. The ball of the thumb is ideal for shaping the inside of a bowl

Thumb pressure must be reasonably strong to begin with but be reduced drastically at the rim to prevent excessive increase in the diameter of the top. When throwing a bowl, it is important to create height before width so the wall must now be lifted as for a cylinder, taking great care not to lose the inside curve profile by bending the fingers of the supporting left hand to match it. The wall will eventually be squeezed outwards to form the large mouth of the bowl so that the wall must be made progressively thicker towards the top. Creating width will also cause loss in height, so the lift should take the clay to a greater height than that required for the finished bowl. Once this height has been attained, the bowl can be finally shaped by drawing the clay outwards and upwards, using the same lifting action. Wheel speed should be reduced as the bowl grows wider and centrifugal force increases (Figure 4.8).

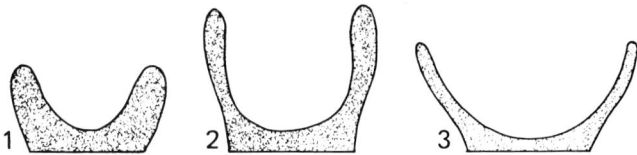

Figure 4.8. Stages in the throwing of a bowl

A careful watch must be kept on the shape of the bowl and pressures adjusted accordingly, especially towards the top edge. It is difficult to gather in the mouth of a bowl which has become too wide. The quicker a bowl can be thrown, the better since a very wet wall is more prone to collapse. When completed, the base of the outer side can be trimmed with the side-tool and the bowl removed from the wheel. A bowl is more easily distorted during this process than a cylindrical pot. Large bowls, as will be indicated later, are best thrown on a batt but smaller ones can be slid from the wheel onto a wetted board held in the left hand.

Shallow bowls can be thrown by adding one further operation. The left palm and extended fingers are turned to face the bowl and used as a support for the outer wall whilst

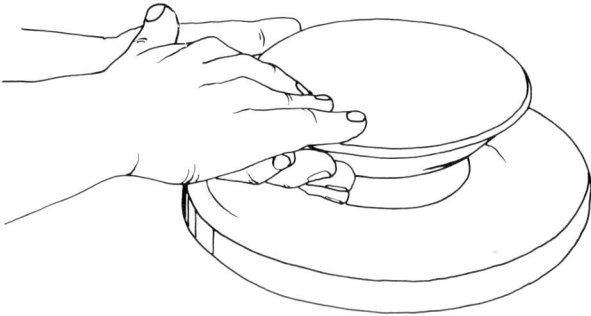

Figure 4.9. Lowering the wall to produce a shallow bowl

the extended fingers of the right hand match this action on the inside. Both hands are then moved simultaneously outwards and upwards which will serve to lower the wall (Figure 4.9). There is a limit to the extent to which a bowl may be flattened. If the lowering is taken too far, the sides will completely collapse (Figure 4.10).

Throwing a bottle-shape

Bottle-shapes are more difficult to control than the two shapes previously described and should not be attempted until the student has become reasonably proficient in the throwing of the cylinder. A bottle-shape begins life in the same manner as the cylinder, but having a narrow top it makes considerable sense to modify the cylindrical form to that of an open-ended funnel. There is no point in throwing a

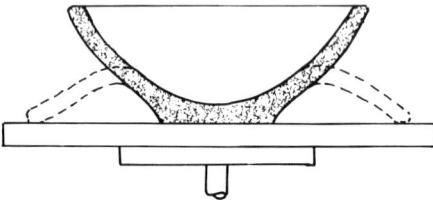

Figure 4.10. The result of lowering the wall too far

wide top which will subsequently have to be narrowed. The top opening must, however, be large enough to accommodate the left hand or throwing will not be possible.

First of all the belly of the pot should be shaped as this is impossible once the top has been narrowed. The next stage is to narrow the top by throwing the shoulder inwards, taking care to maintain a graceful line. Final gathering in and shaping of the bottle neck is achieved by a process known as collaring. The last two fingers of each hand are bent into the

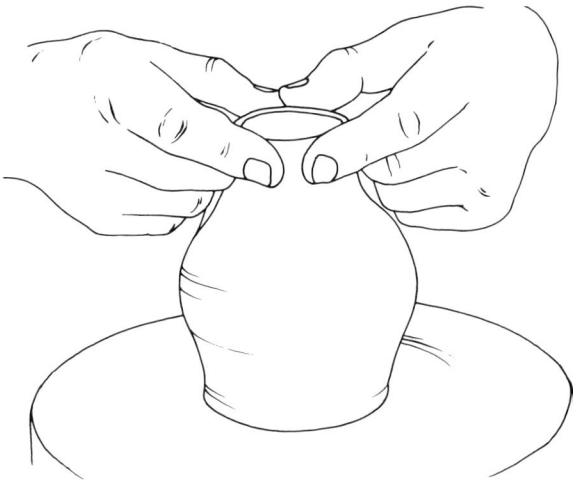

Figure 4.11. Position of the fingers for gathering-in (collaring) a bottle neck

palms, the index fingers bent sufficiently to bring into play that portion of the fingers located between the first and second joints. The index fingers and thumbs are, at the same time, extended. The clay is then 'strangled' by the two first fingers and thumbs and the cranked index fingers spread evenly around it. Slight pressure is brought to bear on the clay at the spring of the neck and the hands slowly raised (without further pressure) to the top, in the line of the required shape (Figure 4.11).

The restrictive action of collaring will cause a thickening of the wall and must be followed by a limited lift to thin it once more. Collaring and thinning are then alternated until the required neck size is obtained. Wheel speed should be increased as the circumference decreases. A very narrow opening may prove too small to allow the entry of the left hand finger, in which case it may be necessary to substitute a brush handle or some similar object for the final gathering (Figure 4.12).

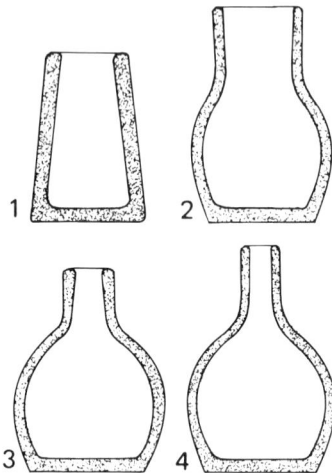

Figure 4.12. Stages in the throwing of a bottle

Large bottle-shapes, such as cider jars, require considerable control – too sudden a shoulder can quite easily cause the complete upper portion to fall.

Composite pots

Large pots with sudden, very flat, shoulder changes, such as the cider jar mentioned above, are sometimes thrown in two sections which are joined when leather-hard with slip and modelled together. If the assembled pot is then recentred and held on the wheel, an extra band of clay can be spun around the joint to give continuity to the whole or, if the wall is sufficiently thick, the pot can be lightly turned as one unit. Lining up one section with another can be made easier if a

Figure 4.13. Constructing a tall composite pot

flange is turned on the lower portion and the upper section turned to sit into it (Figure 4.13). Very tall pots can be built up in a similar fashion, but a full-size drawing is necessary to ensure that the two halves follow a common line.

Repetition throwing

When throwing a set of bowls or other pots it is a good idea to pre-set callipers to the basic diameter sizes and to indicate salient heights of the profile on a hardboard measure. Pot gauges are provided with some wheels which can be pre-set and the pots thrown against them (Figure 4.14).

Above all, it is important to start each pot with the same quantity of weighed-out clay and to ensure that the initial base diameter and thickness is always identical. A matching

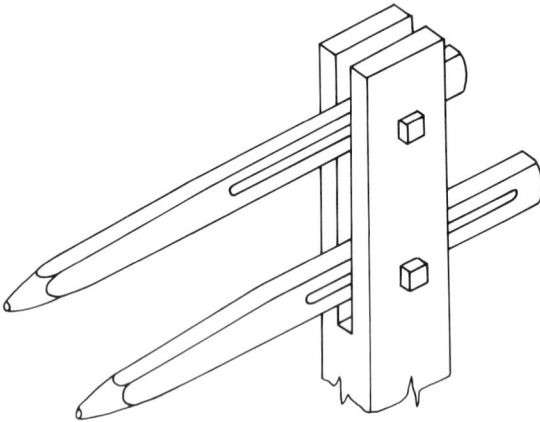

Figure 4.14. Pot gauges behind the wheel to indicate height and diameters for the purpose of repetition throwing

set of items should always be thrown at one session and the same sequence of movements repeated. Memory of the rhythm of making would be disturbed by a long interval between one pot and the next in a set.

Throwing a flat-bottomed dish

This follows the usual throwing sequence, but after the initial opening has been made with the right thumb, the second movement to widen it must be exaggerated and the clay pulled back horizontally to create the large flat base. The sides are then raised and shaped as in a normal pot (Figure 4.15).

If a thickened rim is required, the top of the wall can be well-thinned, levelled, and completely rolled over to sit on the outside edge. To do this hold the index finger of the left hand against the outside of the wall about ½ inch (12 mm) down from the top and roll the clay above it down over this finger with the index finger of the right hand until it forms a

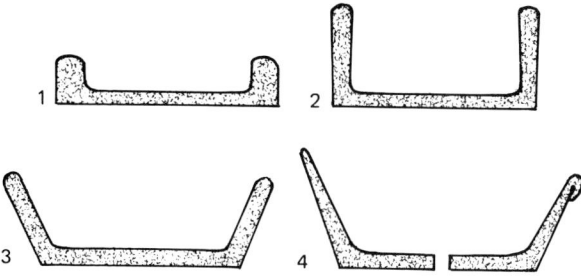

Figure 4.15. Throwing a flat dish

hook-shape. Then pinch both the wall and the turned-over portion between the index finger and thumb of the left hand and complete the fold-down; no air must be trapped between the two (Figure 4.16).

Small dishes can be made directly on the wheel, but a large one will need to be thrown on a batt.

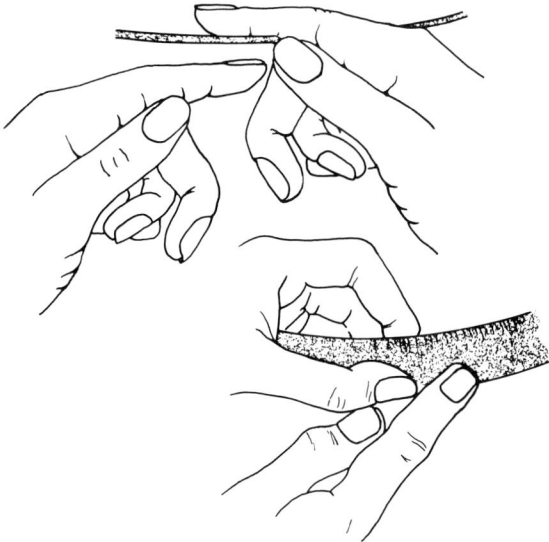

Figure 4.16. Turning over a top to form a thick rim

Oval dishes

Round, flat-bottomed dishes can be converted, with a little ingenuity, into oval shapes. The conversion must be made at the soft, leather-hard stage when the pot is free from the board. A thin section of clay, shaped in the form of a long slender curved diamond, is cut out of the centre of the base.

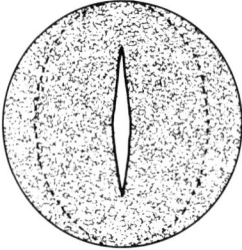

Figure 4.17. Converting a flat round dish to an oval by cutting out a slender rounded diamond in the base

Each side of the excision is coated with slip after which the two sides of the pot can be carefully squeezed together with cupped hands, until the gap made by the removal of the clay is once more fully closed (Figure 4.17). The joint should be made good by thorough luting on both inside and outside.

Throwing on a batt

Very large bowls are best thrown on a batt to avoid distortion when removed wet from the wheel. Batts can be cast in plaster of Paris and turned true before hardening or they can be cut from ⅝ inch (15 mm) or ¾ inch (19 mm) waterproof plywood or blockboard, and should be of the same diameter as the wheel head. Spin a thin layer of fairly soft clay evenly over the wheel and then make a concentric ridge with the finger tip, placing the dampened batt centrally over it. Give the batt a few bangs with the clenched fists to create a strong suction which will hold it firmly to the wheel. The bowl can then be thrown on the batt and when completed, the suction broken and the batt lifted free with the bowl still in place. The pot must be cut free from the batt as soon as it can be handled to avoid shrinkage cracks developing in the base.

Throwing of covered pots

Simple sit-in lid
This is quite simply a small thrown bowl with a narrow thickened base from which the knob can eventually be turned. In other words, it is thrown upside down. The top

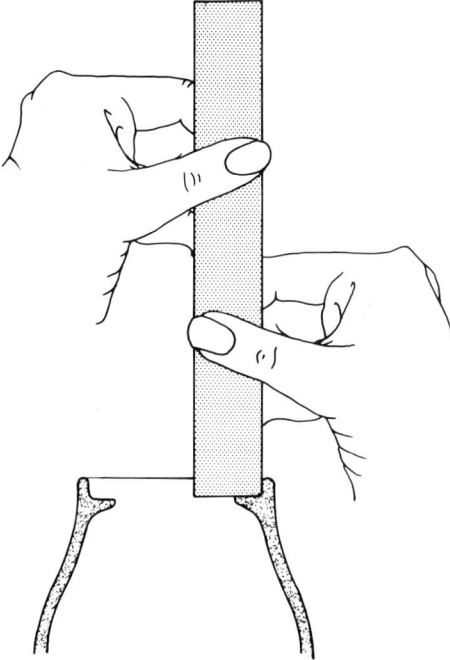

Figure 4.18. Using a boxwood ruler to square the flange on the top of a pot wall

edge of the pot must be modified to provide a seating for the lid by the creation of a flange. The pot wall must be left a trifle thicker to allow for this and to ensure that it is running perfectly true. If necessary, it should be levelled with the pricker. The flange can be made either with the thumb or finger of the left hand, or by gradually feeding down the end of a short wooden ruler or slate held in the same manner as that described for squaring the inside corners of the cylinder (page 25). The wrists should be kept well up against the body to prevent any lateral movement during the formation of the flange (Figure 4.18). Callipers should be set to about ⅛ inch (3 mm) less than the outer diameter of the flange (to allow for two thicknesses of glaze) as used to check the size of mouth of the thrown lid (Figure 4.19).

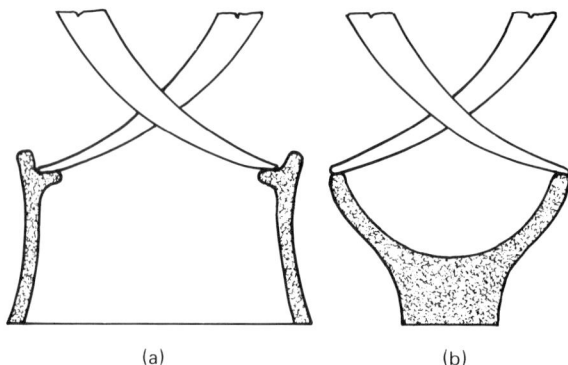

(a)   (b)

Figure 4.19.   Using the callipers to check sizes of (a) pot and (b) lid

It must be emphasised that, when making a covered pot of any design, it is vitally important that both pot and lid are thrown at the same time, so that both shrink evenly and will therefore continue to fit one another.

Flanged lid
Modification of the pot is not necessary for this type of lid since it is designed to incorporate a flange which will sit on the pot wall. This is useful if a design calls for an over-hanging lid. This type of lid is made by throwing a small bowl on an extended base as before but leaving the walls quite thick and rather taller than required. A collar is now made by allowing the rim of the bowl to run lightly between left-hand finger on the inside and the thumb on the outside

Figure 4.20. The action of throwing a flange on a lid

and simultaneously pressing both inwards and downwards with the side of the right thumb to form a ledge which will eventually sit on the top of the pot (Figure 4.20). The angle can be sharpened with the square end of the slate or ruler. The remaining inner wall of clay is now thrown and raised to form a collar, the size of which must be checked against a calliper measurement of the inside diameter of the pot allowing, as before, for two thicknesses of glaze (Figure 4.21).

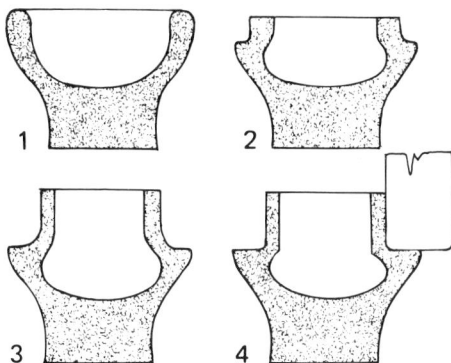

Figure 4.21. Stages in the throwing of a flanged lid

Adjustments to size and collar height can easily be made at this stage. The diameter of the outside of the lid must be that required in the finished pot. A collared lid is less likely to slip off in use.

Flanged pot and flanged lid

For articles which are to be tilted, such as teapots, a flange is made both on the pot itself and on the lid. Throwing lid and pot will be a combination of the skills already acquired inn two previous tye.careful cliperasurments need to be taken; the collar must be a loose fit inside the inner edge of the pot flange, and the diameter of the lid a 'glaze fit', on the outer flange wall. Flange widths on both pot and lid must also be compatible.

Flush lids

From a storage point of view, it is often convenient to design a pot with a flush lid and if it is in constant use there is less danger of the knob being broken. There are many styles, and in similar fashion to the lids already described, they can sit in a pot flange, on a lid flange, or be a combination of both. Flush lids are usually thrown the right way up so that the inset knob is thrown and not turned.

Centre a lump of clay on the wheelhead and shape it to form a thick disc, roughly equalent in diamer to the ished ld. Then make a running groove into the disc with the right thumb, allowing sufficient standing clay to remain at the centre for subsequent shaping of the knob, sufficient thickness of base to form the bottom of the lid, and enough thickness at the outer edge from which to raise the outer wall. Now lift this wall above the level of the clay and make it of such a diameter to fit loosely into the mouth of the pot. The top edge of this outer wall should then be turned outwards to form a right-angled flange. This operation is best accomplished by rolling the clay over the index finger of the right hand, held against the outer wall with the first two fingers of the left, and finishing it with the finger and thumb of the right hand. The width of this overhang must be adjusted, with the aid of the callipers, to that required either

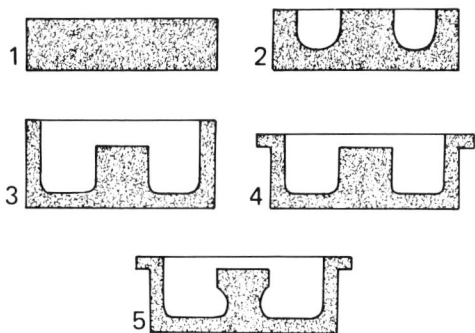

Figure 4.22. Stages in the throwing of a flush flanged lid

for a straight pot overlap or to sit inside a flanged top. It may be necessary to remove some of the clay with the pricker. The knob can now be shaped from the 'island' of clay left at the centre (Figure 4.22).

A flush lid which combines a strap handle can be made by combining a small thrown bowl with a rolled-out slab of clay (see page 78) cut to the correct diameter and pierced with two half-moons on either side of a suitably sized web to serve as a handle. When both sections are leather-hard, the bowl is luted beneath the piercings (Figure 4.23).

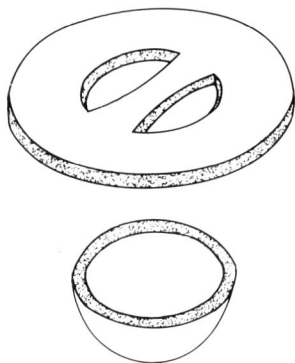

Figure 4.23. A flush lid comprising a slab of rolled-out clay and a thrown bowl.

43

Sit-over lid
This takes the form of a small dish thrown with a sufficiently large mouth to fit over a vertical gallery thrown on the pot. Such a lid must fit very loosely to allow for any distortion in the shape of the pot during firing (Figure 4.24).

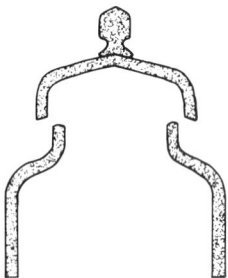

Figure 4.24. A sit-on lid

Designing a lid
A lid should harmonise with the body of the pot and cmplement its shape, so that an unbroken line is presented by both. Careful thought should also be given to the knob. From a functional point of view, it must be easy and safe to grip and if large, for example on a vegetable dish or casserole, it is wise to hollow it slightly to make for lightness and a safer passage in the kiln. In many instances it is a good rule to think of the shape of the knob as being an inverted reflection of the pot itself. This shaping is completed by turning, when the lid is thrown, upside down (see page 51).

Spouts and lips

The simplest provision for pouring is the lip which can be pulled from the side of a thrown pot as soon as it has been made. The first two fingers of the left hand are opened to form a 'V' and allowed to rest vertically against the outer and upper edge of the pot (Figure 4.25a). The right index finger is then used in an upwards, outwards and rounded motion to

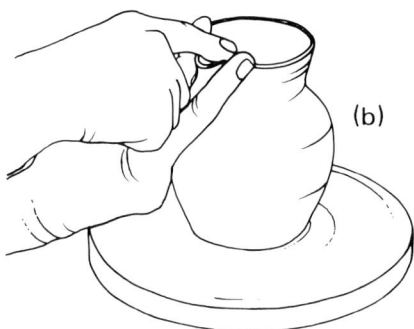

Figure 4.25. Pulling a lip on a jug

pull the clay from the inside between the two extended fingers which act as a stop to prevent outward movement of the remainder of the rim (Figure 4.25*b*).

This pulling action should end with a second inward curve to prevent liquid dripping from the lip after pouring. Larger lips can be added to a pot when it is leather-hard and can be cut from a stumpy spout thrown on the wheel.

Throwing a spout
This is a further example of the throwing of a bottle-shape (see page 32). The throwing begins by lifting a tapered wall which can have a straight, convex, concave, or bellied-out

Figure 4.26. Some thrown spout shapes

form, reminiscent of the old bottle-neck kilns. It should have a sufficiently spacious base to hold enough liquid to build up a pouring pressure and so ensure a good flow (Figure 4.26).

Spouts are quite often thrown at the top of a larger piece of clay and cut off using the pricker (Figure 4.27). It is a good

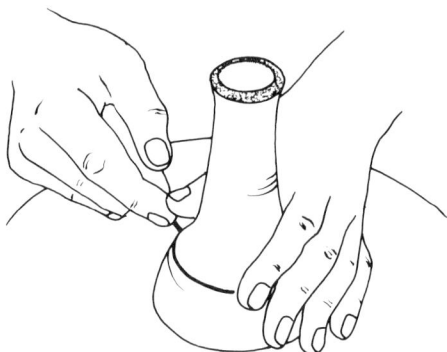

Figure 4.27. Cutting off a thrown spout using the pricker

idea to throw more than one spout for any particular job so that a spare is available to experiment with when carrying out the final fitting to the pot. With a little care, the wet, freshly-thrown spout can be slightly bent over to help match the natural curve of the pot.

5

Turning

The process of turning clay is similar to that used for shaping wood, indeed, industrial ware is still turned on a horizontal lathe. The studio potter uses the wheel as a vertical lathe. Turning is carried out when the pot has become leather-hard and the clay must be cut and not scraped. Therefore turning tools must be well maintained with good cutting edges.

It is customary to provide a pot with a foot ring for several reasons. When fired, the base of a pot is liable to bulge which can seriously impair stability. However, if the pot rests on a foot this is not significant. Furthermore, the removal of clay to form the foot makes for a light base. The foot also serves an even more vital function. If left unglazed, it prevents an unstilted pot from becoming welded to the kiln shelf during the glaze fire.

Turning the base of a pot

The first task must be to centre the pot mouth downwards on the wheel face. An experienced potter will place it as near centre as possible and make it turn perfectly true by a few well-judged taps with the left hand. The beginner will find the concentric rings, which are scored on some wheel heads, useful. Alternatively, one or two pencil lines can be spun onto a plain steel wheel. A measure of trial and error will at first be inevitable, but the student is urged to practise 'tap centring' with a spare pot as the skill can save much valuable time. To check whether a pot is centred spin the wheel and hold out a steadied index finger. It should touch the pot all the way round, if not, you can see which direction to move it.

Once centred, the pot is held in position on the wheel with three well-spaced dabs of clay. These are fully stuck to the wheel but merely brace the pot. A piece of wood about $4 \times 1 \times \frac{3}{4}$ inch ($1220 \times 25 \times 19$ mm) is necessary to support the tool. This 'rest stick' is held by tucking it under the left arm, allowing the far end to find a firm anchor at a suitable point – a back corner of the wheel is often convenient. It is held in this position with the left hand and used somewhat in the manner of a painter's maulstick. Some potters prefer to fix a flat piece of wood to the near end of the stick so that it can be

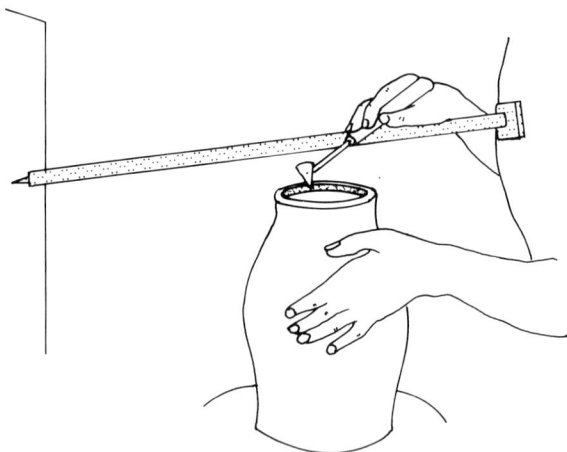

Figure 5.1. Turning a pot with the aid of a maulstick

held in position by pressure against the body (Figure 5.1). The tool must be held at such an angle that it removes a continuous clay shaving. If it is not convenient in every case to use the support stick, the tool can be held steady by allowing the pot to spin freely within the left hand and the tool braced with the left thumb (Figure 5.2).

Before beginning to turn any pot, examine it carefully, firstly to get some idea of the outside line so that it can be satisfactorily resolved by the outer turning of the base, and secondly to assess the thickness available for turning in the lower clay wall. It is also important to estimate the thickness

Figure 5.2. Using the left hand as a support when turning the base of a pot

of the base in order to ascertain the amount of clay which can safely be cut away to form the ring. To tell how thick the base is hold the pot up to the ear and tap the outside of the base; a resonant sound indicates a thin base and a dull sound a thick one. Since turning will affect the ultimate diameter of the foot, the outside must be turned first, preferably starting with a hoop tool and finishing with a normal tool which possesses the appropriate profile. It is helpful to complete the turning with a small concave curve if this can be happily married to the dominant line of the pot. This is a tremendous help as a finger grip when the pot finally has to be glazed (Figure 5.3).

When turning the outside is complete, the hoop tool can once again be used to check that the base is perfectly flat and to rough out the clay to form the foot ring, working from the centre outwards across a right-hand radius. The ring itself should not be too wide, $^{3}/_{16}$–$^{1}/_{4}$ inch (4–6 mm) being about right, though much depends on the type and size of pot. The hollowing is completed with a flat, square-ended tool and the ring so formed is lightly bevelled on the inside and given a

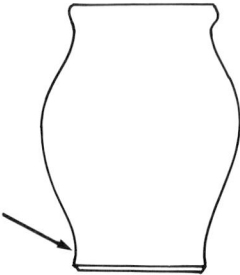

Figure 5.3. A concave curve turned at the pot base

small chamfer on the outer edge. When a foot is being turned on an earthenware pot which will be stilted when packed into the glaze kiln, care must be taken to ensure that the depth of the 'well' cut into the base is not greater than the overall height of the stilt on which it may have to rest if a stilt is not available to fit the foot. A well thrown pot requires no further turning and indiscriminate paring of the sides can ruin its character. Some pots, however, are designed to be fully turned and are thrown to a basic shape with the walls left thicker than normal for the purpose. This technique makes it possible to incorporate embellishments such as grooves or mouldings. The surface can be highly polished if, after turning, it is burnished with a smooth modelling tool or the flat surface of a bone folder.

Turning the foot on a bottle-shape

It is impossible to balance a narrow-necked bottle upside down on the wheelhead. To enable a foot to be turned, the potter must resort to a clay turning-ring which will serve as a chuck. It is a good idea to throw a number of rings of varying size and to keep them ready for use in the damp box. The ring is centred on the wheel, fixed in place with a few pieces of clay and the inner diameter checked with a turning tool to make sure it is running true. The bottle is now inverted so that the neck hangs down into the ring and the body rests on the ring itself. Getting it to run true with the centred ring is a

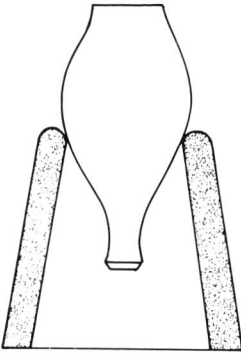

Figure 5.4. Supporting a bottle whilst turning the foot

question of trial and error but it helps to estimate the direction of error if the bottom of the bottle is viewed at eye level when spinning. When running true, the bottle is fixed to the ring with a few dabs of clay and the base turned in the usual way (Figure 5.4).

Turning and fitting lids

When throwing a normal lid, a thick narrow mass of clay was left at the base (see page 39). After hardening, the lid is centred the correct way up on the wheel and the knob turned from this surplus clay. No specific instructions can be given for this, since knobs will all be of different shapes, but it is good policy to begin by turning a cylinder of the maximum diameter needed and to complete the final shaping from this. Undercutting to form the grip ledge will need special care but a piece of old clock spring (which has so many uses) can be bent to any required diameter and will do the job admirably when the round-ended turning tool proves to be too large.

Should the lid itself have been thrown a trifle too large and need adjustment, this must be dealt with before attempting

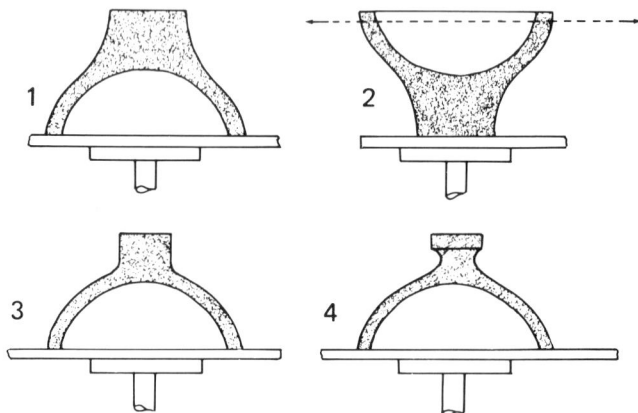

Figure 5.5. Correcting lid size and turning the knob

to form the knob. The lid can be centred the correct way up to level the top and then reversed and any necessary adjustments made (Figure 5.5). A spoonway can be cut into the lid, if desired, so that a spoon can remain inside the pot whilst the lid is still in position.

Common problems

A *pulled lip* on a jug can prevent it from sitting comfortably on the wheel. It is a good plan to support this lip with a bolster of soft clay.

If the pot *lifts repeatedly* during turning, it is usually an indication, either that it has been allowed to dry too much or that the wheel itself is too dry. The cure lies in redampening the wheel and the pot rim. The problem can be exacerbated by blunt turning tools or by taking too deep a cut, both of which create excessive friction on the clay and encourage lift.

Chatter, which manifests itself as the formation of vertical corrugations in the clay surface, can be the result of insufficient support being afforded to the tool, a pot which has become too hard, or a tool which has been made excessively sharp. Continued turning serves only to emphasise the ridges. It can generally be cured by dampening the surface thoroughly and holding a wide, flat tool diagonally across the ridges.

6

Handles, spouts and accessories

Designing a handle

'Handle with care' is a motto which is as applicable to pottery as it is to the cabinet maker for in either craft a badly chosen handle can seriously mar an otherwise excellent piece of work. Consideration must be given to the following: A handle must suit the type of ware to which it is to be attached. One produced from a plaster of Paris mould would

Figure 6.1. The handle must appear to 'grow' organically from the pot

not fit well on a large vigorously thrown jug. A handle must be functional – comfortable to handle and fixed in a position to give a well-balanced hold and pour. It should merge with the general form of the pot and grow organically from it (Figure 6.1). It should not be overlarge in cross-section. The strength of a handle can be measured by the quality of bond made between it and the pot and not by its thickness.

Making handles

Pulled handles
This is the type usually associated with the work of the studio potter. Form a piece of well wedged clay into a thick roll and hold vertically in the left hand over a bucket of water with the fingers curled around the back and the thumb held across the front. Now wet the clay and pull downwards by stroking with the wet fingers and thumb of the right hand which should be arranged in a position below and exactly opposite

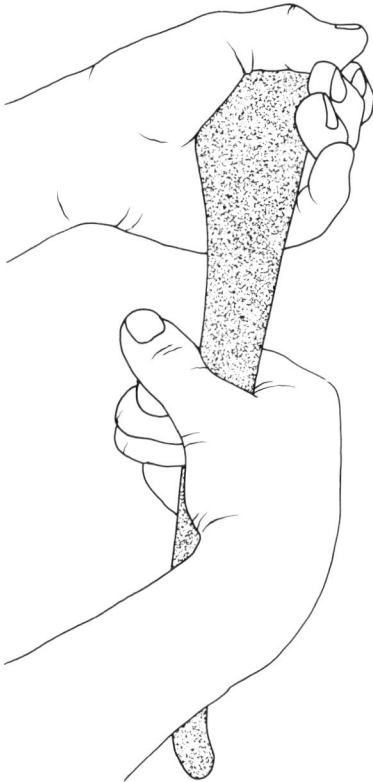

Figure 6.2. Pulling a handle

the left hand. A slight pressure must be exerted both inwards and downwards and the pull made to follow a curved path away from the body. This stroking action must be continued until a satisfactory cross-section has been achieved, both the clay and the right hand being kept well lubricated with water. The process requires considerable practice to judge the exact amount of pressure and pull which it is safe to apply and the student must not be discouraged if several abortive efforts are made. It is essential to get to know the feel of the clay and to maintain an even series of strokes. If too much pressure is applied, especially at the lower end of the roll, the clay can quite easily break off and the gradual thinning from top to bottom, which is one of the great advantages of a pulled handle, will be lost (Figure 6.2).

The actual cross-section of the handle can be regulated by varying the relative positions of the right hand fingers and thumb; the closer they are brought together the more oval and flatter will be the cross-section. The tip of the thumb, too, can be brought into play to create a handle which has a concave face (Figure 6.3). When pulling is complete, the

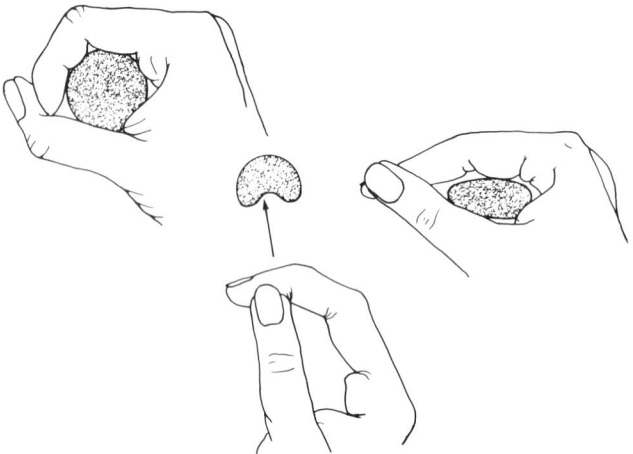

Figure 6.3. The cross-section of a pulled handle can be varied by adjusting the position of the fingers and thumb

handle should be hung on the edge of the bench to dry off. It must not be allowed to dry to the full leather-hard state and must be fixed whilst the clay is still plastic.

Cut off the thick end at a chosen point and stick this with slip onto its correct upper position on the pot, the point of attachment having been previously marked by scratching. Now cut the length of handle required and fix the thin end with slip onto the lower point of attachment, pressing it into position. The handle, still being in a plastic state will assume its own natural curve, the length of handle and distance between the two points of attachment being the deciding factors. An experienced potter will often fix the roll of clay to its correct upper position and actually pull it whilst it is in situ, finally pinching it off to the correct length and pressing on the lower end. The bond between the handle and the pot must be well pressed and modelled by the fingers, the sides of the joint being smoothed to merge with the wall. The finger marks and the splayed handle edges, which result from the pressing-on, can be attractive features.

Wire-pulled handles
Handles of uniform length and section can be made by using wire loops. Some 17 or 18 swg galvanised iron wire is pulled tightly around a circular former which is held securely in a vice. The two ends are then tightly twisted in front of it until the length of twist is about 4½ inches (115 mm) (Figure 6.4). It is a good idea to make a collection of such wires with varying loop sizes which can be kept for general use. It is also possible to modify the initial loop with a pair of round-nosed pliers into an oval or flat section.

To make the wire-pulled handle, first form some well-wedged clay into a brick shape. Then dip the wire loop into water, and hold it vertically against the end of the brick with the twisted portion comfortably held in the palm of the right hand and the loop well supported at its outer front point by the index finger. Hold the brick of clay firm with the finger and thumb of the left hand and pull the wire loop smartly through the length of the clay, making sure that it does not twist as it is pulled. In most cases, the handle which is formed

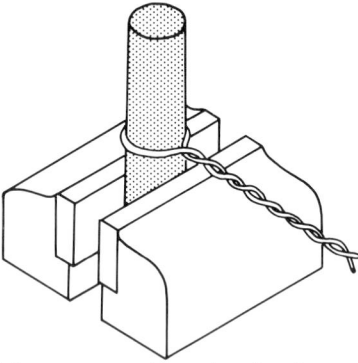

Figure 6.4.   Making a handle wire

by this action will emerge from the opposite end with the wire but if this fails to happen, the two sides of the clay can be pulled to either side and the handle lifted out (Figure 6.5).

Place the finished handle on a sheet of paper covering a flat board in a position as near as possible to that of its final shape. If the turned pot which it is to fit is held immediately

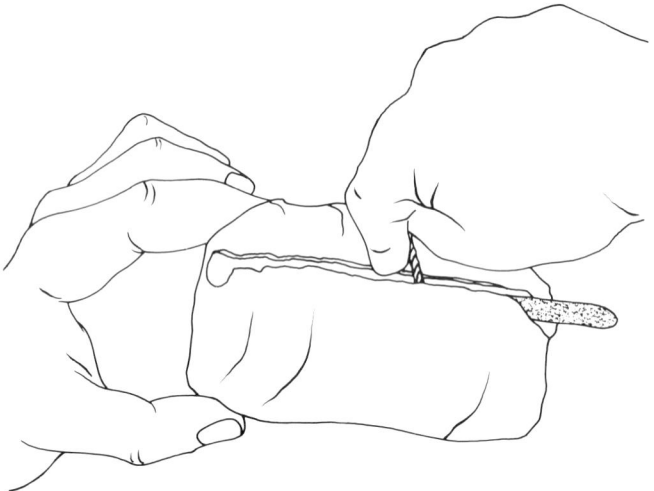

Figure 6.5.   Using the wire to produce a handle from a lump of clay

over it, the required curvature can be judged more easily. For repetitive pieces it is wise to make a series of identical pencil drawings of the required shape on the paper sheet so that the newly-pulled handles can be lined up with them.

A fettle line will be evident on a wire-pulled handle at the point where the two ends of wire were first twisted together. It should always be arranged for this line to be on the inside of the curve so that it can be lightly pared away after the handle has been fixed. Since it is of an even cross-section, a wire-pulled handle is allowed to dry more before fixing. The two ends are trimmed with a knife and fitted to the profile of the pot before being painted with slip, luted and modelled to the basic form.

Making handles on the wheel
Full cylindrical or tapered handles suitable for fixing to ovenware, pipkins or traditional coffee pots, can be thrown on the wheel in similar manner to a spout. If the upper walls

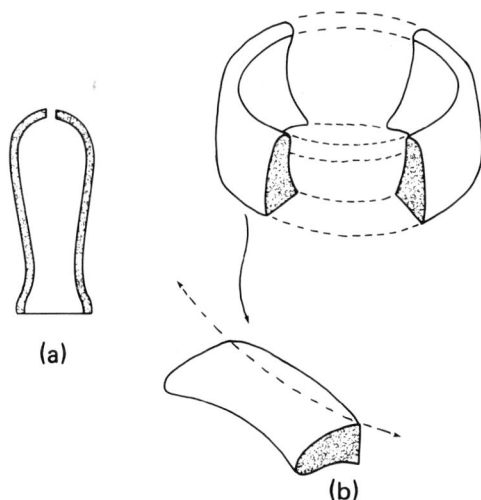

Figure 6.6.   Two types of thrown handle.
(a) Cylindrical – note the air vent at the top.
(b) Method of cutting lug handles from a thrown ring

are gathered over to make a domed end, it is important to ensure that a hole is left to vent the inner cavity since air inside would, on expansion during firing, cause a serious blowout.

Side lug handles can be cut, when leather-hard, from a suitably shaped clay ring thrown on the wheel. This ensures perfect matching (Figure 6.6). The inner edge must be trimmed to suit the curve of the pot before fixing.

Pressed handles
Small handles, such as might be needed for a set of teacups, can be produced from a press mould. The technique is fully described on page 74.

Cut-out handles
These can be cut from rolled out slabs of clay and are suitable for attachment to slab-built ware. Two narrow clay strips can even be plaited together if decorative contrast is thought to be desirable.

Thumb grips
A small quantity of clay added at the head of a handle can be moulded or subsequently carved to form a thumb grip or

Figure 6.7. A thumb grip modelled to a jug handle

stop. This can be a functional feature on a heavy piece as well as adding to the general form (Figure 6.7).

Adding accessories

A careful eye must be kept on the alignment of added accessories. It is all too easy, when concentrating on accurate fitting and modelling, to fix a spout or lip in a position not diametrically opposite the handle.

60

Fixing an added lip

An added lip can either be cut from a thrown stumpy spout, or hand-bent from a piece of rolled out clay cut to the shape of a section of a developed truncated cone (Figure 6.8). A trial template can be cut from a piece of paper. In either case it must be accurately trimmed with a small knife to a good fit

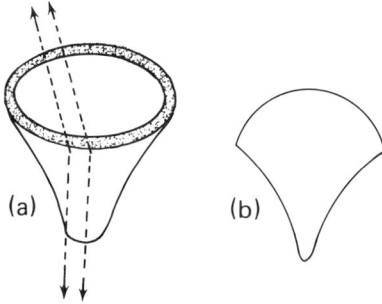

Figure 6.8. (a) Cutting an applied lip from a thrown stumpy cone. (b) Typical development for an applied spout cut from a slab of clay

with the pot before being joined on with slip and luted. The waste clay from the pot on the inner side of the lip can then be completely cut away or, if desired, a portion of the rim can be left. This will do much to prevent distortion when fired (Figure 6.9).

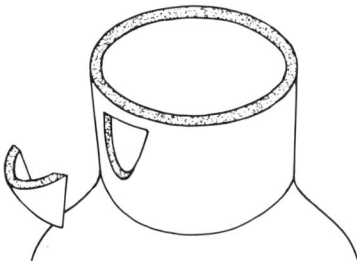

Figure 6.9. A lip fitted to maintain an unbroken rim

61

In certain cases, it may be necessary to cut grid holes to serve as a strainer. The inner side of the joint must be luted and smoothed, ensuring that any ledge, at the pouring point, which might hinder the flow of fluid, is well resolved. It is far easier to fix the lip before, rather than after, cutting out the waste.

Fixing a pipe spout

First cut the spout from its thrown base with a sharp knife. The angle of cut must be assessed with regard to the final inclination of the spout and the cut end carefully modified to match the profile of the pot. The spout must be accurately fitted to avoid air being trapped in the joint. If the base walls of the thrown spout are found to be too thick, they can be pared with a knife to an acceptable size. The top of the spout must always be level with the mouth of the pot, otherwise liquid will flow from the spout before the pot is full. Spouts are normally fitted quite low on teapots and relatively high on the traditional coffee pot. This used to be so that the drink could be decanted from the top of the settled coffee grounds, but nowadays, with the more widespread use of coffee bags and percolators, the pot is merely used to serve the beverage, so that this functional feature need not dictate the spout position.

When fitted hold the spout in place and draw a light line around it with a sharp pencil. Remove the spout and draw a second line inside the first at a distance equivalent to the thickness of the spout wall. The area of clay inside this second line can then either be completely removed or a grid of regularly spaced holes can be cut with a hole piercer used in the manner of a hand drill (Figure 6.10).

The holes must not, under any circumstances, be pushed through with a blunt-pointed instrument as this would cause the webs of clay between the holes to break. Any loose pieces of clay left on either side of the holes must be removed, otherwise they will interfere with the flow of liquid and cause problems when glazing.

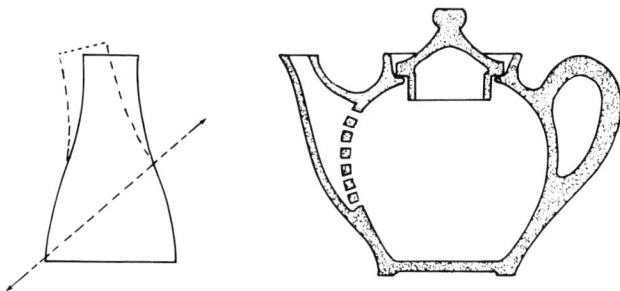

Figure 6.10. Fixing a teapot spout

When this has been done the spout can be joined on with slip and thoroughly modelled to the pot. A little extra clay can be added, where necessary, to soften the junction and maintain a good flowing line. If no grid has been left, it should be possible to deal with the inside of the joint as described earlier. Finally, trim the spout at the mouth to the correct length and to any required angle, smoothing the cut edge. It is sometimes advantageous to 'pull' a tiny lip as an aid to pouring. Spouts cut off at an angle will sometimes tend to twist in the fire but it is a risk which must be taken.

Provisions for added cane handles

This type of handle is sometimes fitted to articles, such as teapots or biscuit barrels, by means of two small clay strips or rolls fitted on either side. They can be pulled with a wire or simply be shaped rolls of clay (Figure 6.11).

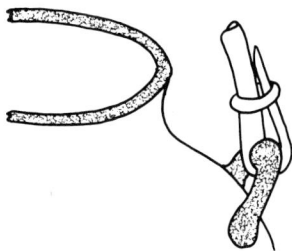

Figure 6.11. Provision for the fitting of a cane handle

7

Plaster of Paris moulds

Two grades of plaster are usually quoted in a catalogue. High grade potter's plaster of standard density is used for normal mould making. *High density* plaster usually listed is used mainly in the preparation of block and case moulds which are described later in this chapter.

Mixing plaster of Paris

It is essential to use the plaster in the correct proportion of 5 pounds (2.7 kg) to 3 pints (1.7 litres) of water since the final mould must be of optimum strength and porosity. Careful mixing is important to avoid the formation of air bubbles and

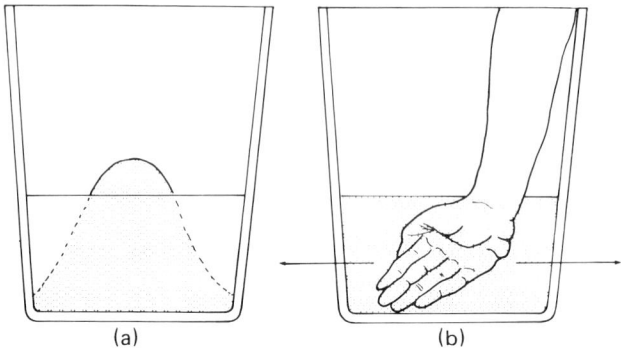

Figure 7.1. Mixing plaster: (a) The pile of plaster in the bucket. (b) Agitating plaster without creating unnecessary air bubbles

lumps. Measure out the water in a bucket and sprinkle the weighed plaster into it. When this has been completed a small 'hill' will have built up. Leave the mixture for a little while to allow the water to permeate the plaster. During this time the hill will gradually disappear. When no more air bubbles appear, agitate the liquid by moving one hand, held palm upwards, backwards and forwards on the bottom of the bucket, until a homogeneous mix is obtained (Figure 7.1).

A careful watch must now be kept as setting is rapid and pouring must take place when the setting process is about to begin. A good test is to draw a finger lightly across the surface of the plaster. If this leaves a definite wake, it is ready to pour. If left too long, the plaster ceases to be mobile.

Simple drain moulds

This procedure is best explained by reference to a specific dish, as illustrated (Figure 7.2).

The first stage in preparing a plaster mould of the dish is to model its form upside down in solid clay, on a flat board.

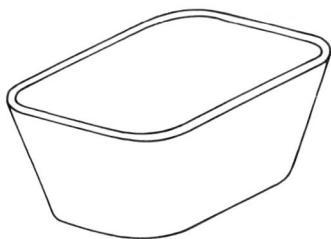

Figure 7.2. The specimen of a cast dish

Templates are then prepared in card: one of the plan of the mouth (A) and one of the side elevation (B) as an aid to the modelling (Figure 7.3).

If the latter template is cut with tinsnips from tin plate, it can also double as a useful scraper. (An opened-out tin, such as those used to sell dried milk, is a good source of suitable metal.) The clay surface should be given as smooth and

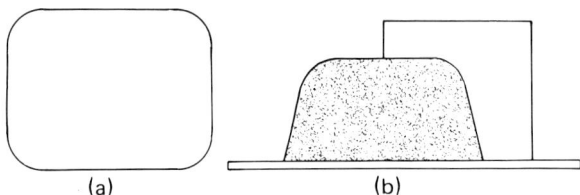

Figure 7.3. The two essential templates for making the
initial clay form. (a) Plan. (b) Side elevation

accurate a finish as possible, remembering that plaster will
faithfully reproduce every detail.

The next stage is to surround the clay form with a wall to
retain the plaster when poured. It is a good idea to make up a
wooden casting box, as illustrated, using ordinary angle-
brackets, as this can then be used repeatedly for varying sizes
of cast (Figure 7.4). Alternatively, walls can be made of thick

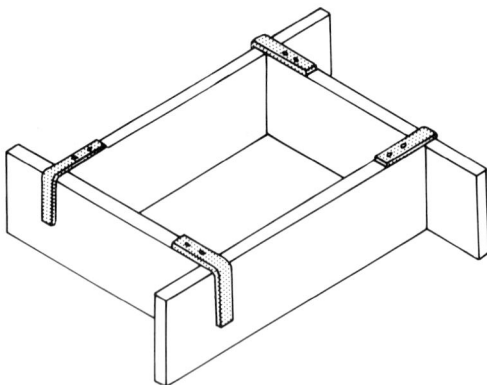

Figure 7.4. Home-made casting box

clay slabs. In either case, care must be taken to seal every
joint with plastic clay as plaster will leak from even the
smallest crack. A good reinforcing roll around the base of the
container should be added.

When all this is completed the plaster is mixed and a
sufficient amount poured into the box to cover the clay shape

66

by about 1¼ inches (32 mm). It is essential to pour gently to ensure that no air bubbles are trapped, especially against the clay core. Above all, avoid splashing. Lifting the board about an inch or so and giving it a gentle bounce back onto the table will help to bring any bubbles, which may have formed, to the surface. The plaster can now be left to set.

An indication that setting is taking place is given by the fact that the surface will become warm to the touch since setting is a chemical process and therefore accompanied by heat. Once cool, the casting box or clay wall can safely be removed. It is advisable to trim the edges of the cast with an old knife. This makes the mould more pleasant to handle and avoids the edges being chipped. Drying out of the plaster will continue and the process can be assisted by removing the clay model, taking great care not to damage the plaster impression. The clay will come away quite cleanly once a grip has been established. The mould is now left to dry and harden.

Casting slip

When dry, a plaster mould is absorbent and it is this property which is exploited in the technique of slip casting. The prepared mould is filled with liquid clay and allowed to stand. The plaster surface absorbs water evenly and a semi-dry layer of clay is thus built up next to it. When this layer is of sufficient thickness, the remaining slip is poured away leaving a hollow clay cast. Ordinary clay slip is not ideal for this purpose as it contains far too much water which means that casting time is lengthy, and the plaster mould soon becomes very damp. A special casting slip is therefore made containing only a little more water than is present in normal plastic clay and yet remains fluid.

Clay particles are held together by the attraction of their electrical charges. These bonds can be broken down by the addition to the water of a small quantity of an alkaline electrolyte. The particles, instead of being held together, become dispersed or deflocculated thus allowing the mixture to become more fluid. For deflocculants, the potter uses sodium carbonate and sodium silicate. Amounts are very critical and differ from one clay body to another. It is therefore vital to keep strictly to the recipe specified by the suppliers.

Sodium silicate is a viscous, treacle-like liquid and the correct amount is best weighed out in a container, the weight of which is already known. If the silicate is found to be too difficult to pour, a little heat will help. One of two density grades may be called for by the recipe, 75°TW (Degrees Twaddell) or 140°TW. The two grades are not interchangeable. Normal plastic or powdered clay may be used but amounts of added water will vary. If plastic clay is used it must be shredded to allow the deflocculants to reach as large a surface area as possible therefore powdered clay is the easier option.

The exact amount of each alkali is weighed out and both are dissolved in a small quantity of hot water before adding to the remainder of the prescribed volume of water contained in a bucket. The powdered clay can then be stirred in, a little at a time. The mixture is allowed to stand for a while and then sieved through a 80–120 mesh lawn. Shredded plastic clay should be placed lightly in the bucket and the water containing the alkalis poured over it. The bucket should be covered and the treated clay left to stand for 24 hours, after which it must be thoroughly churned by hand before sieving. Casting slip is best stored for a few days before use. It should be covered to prevent drying out. A quick stir immediately before pouring is all that is then necessary.

Casting

When completely dried out the plaster mould should be placed on a level surface and the casting slip gently poured in. As the plaster absorbs water the slip level will go down and must be topped up so that the thickness of the wall remains even to the top. How long to leave the slip in the mould can only be decided by personal judgement, but 20

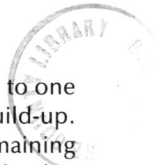

minutes is an average time. Slightly tipping the mould to one side will show roughly the thickness of the clay build-up. When the thickness is thought to be adequate, the remaining slip is slowly, but continuously, poured back into the bucket and the mould left to drain at an angle of about 20 degrees until all the slip has cleared. The mould is then returned to the flat position (Figure 7.5).

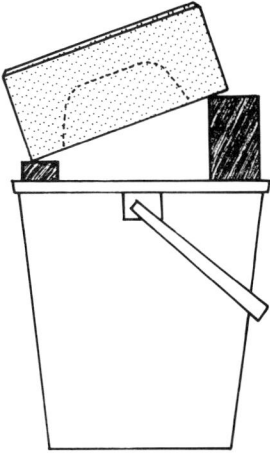

Figure 7.5. The removal of surplus slip from a drain mould

The dish will shrink as it dries and can then be removed by covering the mouth of the mould with a board before inverting the whole. Prior to removal the top should be trimmed level with a palette knife.

A set of identical pieces can easily be made by the casting method. As plaster becomes damper after each pour, if several dishes are made at the same session, the time during which the slip remains in the mould will need to be progressively increased if the thickness of each dish wall is to remain constant. The problem is solved in the pottery industry by making block-and-case moulds. Quite simply, this means taking a cast of the original mould from which numerous copies can be made, all ready for filling with slip at the same time and so guaranteeing standard clay thickness. An examination of the cast dish will probably reveal some irregularity in the top edge. To guard against this, a waste portion is often modelled onto the clay core which will be cast with the main pot and subsequently be removed with a sharp knife. A waste piece will also make 'topping up' unnecessary since the level of slip is unlikely to drop below that of the waste area (Figure 7.6).

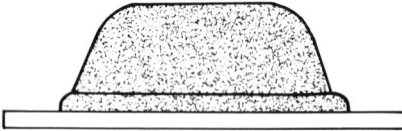

Figure 7.6. A waste portion modelled onto the initial clay form

The dish used in the example could only be removed from its mould because the shape followed a continually enlarging profile. This is a vital concept in casting technique. A mould for a shape in which the line of the side changes direction will need to be made in two separate parts.

Two-piece moulds

As before, the process is best explained by considering a definite example. The initial stage is to produce the vase as a solid entity, preferably with a waste allowance in the form of a tapered plug. Since it is round in section, the desired shape can be roughly formed on the wheel, left to harden and then finished by turning. A vertical dividing line must be plotted on the model. Draw a diameter on the base, and extend vertical lines from its extremities on either side with the aid of a set square and pencil (Figure 7.7). This can be checked at trial points with a pair of callipers.

Now bury the model in a block of soft clay up to the dividing line, leaving the waste end open. Careful modelling

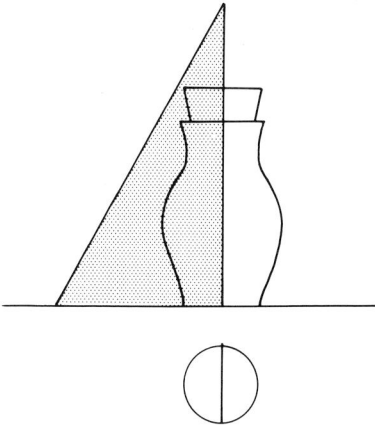

Figure 7.7. Using a set square to draw
a vertical line on a shaped form

is required to ensure a clean edge against the line and a flat
horizontal surface. Now place the casting box accurately
around the block and seal all joints well with clay. Mix
enough plaster to cover the model by about 1½ inches
(38 mm) and pour it in. When the plaster is set, remove the
casting box together with the added block of clay. This will
leave the vase core half-buried in plaster (Figure 7.8).

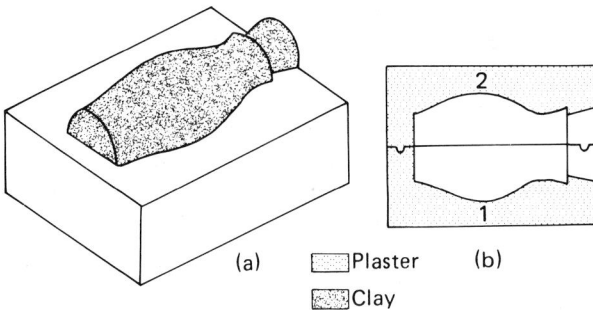

(a) ▢ Plaster (b)
     ▨ Clay

Figure 7.8.   (a) Burying the solid clay core in preparation for
pouring the first plaster section. (b) Both plaster sections
poured

71

To provide for correct register between the two halves of the mould, dome-shaped natch holes must be cut at the corners of the damp plaster. These will be reflected as protrusions in the second half of the mould and can be made by twisting with the handle of an old teaspoon.

Before pouring the second half of plaster, the first half, already cast, must be sealed with soap size to prevent the two portions from adhering. Soap size is prepared by dissolving a lump of soft soap (*Sapo mollis*), about 2 ounces (60 g) in weight, in 8 fluid ounces (12 tablespoonsful) of hot water, to which one or two drops of olive oil have been added. When the solution has cooled it can be bottled and stored until needed. Pour a little of this soap size onto the plaster surface and whip up into a lather, with a brush – an old shaving brush is ideal. Wash the lather off completely and repeat the process twice more. After the last lathering do not wash the surface but remove the lather with a sponge. Now replace the casting box and pour the second half of the mould. Once set, remove the box, separate the two halves and lift out the original solid model. If separation proves difficult, brief immersion in a bucket of water will prove effective.

Before making a clay cast, the two halves of the mould must be securely tied, but otherwise the procedure is identical to that used for the simple dish drain mould. When the cast is removed, the waste portion is trimmed away, either on the wheel or by hand. There will be a distinct line where the two halves of the mould met. This is known as the fettle line and may need cleaning up or fettling.

The number of portions which comprise the mould will increase as the shape becomes more complicated. If, for example, the vase has a turned foot, a temporary clay plug, in the form of a truncated cone, is thrown and accurately turned so that its smaller diameter is equivalent to that of the turned foot. This is held tightly in place against the foot with its large diameter flush with the wall of the casting box. The meeting point between the clay plug and the foot should be lightly sealed with a little clay to prevent plaster from seeping in. A normal two-piece mould is then produced treating the vase core, the top waste portion and the bottom clay plug as one and the same unit. When the plaster has set, the sections are separated, the temporary clay plug removed and the two halves, together with the vase core, reassembled, bound tightly together and placed foot end upwards. Natch holes are cut in the two flat portions on either side and all the exposed uppermost plaster surfaces soap-sized. Finally, a cottle is erected and plaster poured in until the existing plaster is covered to a depth of approximately 1 inch (25 mm) (Figure 7.9).

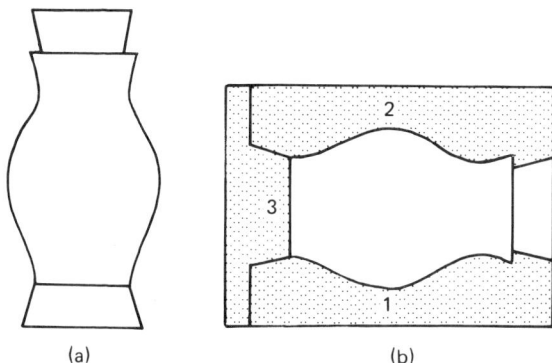

Figure 7.9. Making a 3-piece mould. (a) The master-form has two waste pieces modelled on. (b) The three plaster sections

After setting, the mould is opened and the clay core completely removed. The result is a three-piece assembly which must be bound together before being treated as a normal drain mould.

A teapot which has a flanged top would need yet another section. Details of the production of moulds of this complexity are beyond the brief of a Beginner's Guide, but ability to make a two-piece mould can be usefully employed in the making of small press moulds to produce solid repetitive items such as cup handles or ceramic beads. Supposing, for example, it is decided to add short stumpy legs to a set of the rectangular dishes made in the drain mould already described. One leg would be modelled and a two-piece mould prepared from it, but with both ends, not just one, closed. Once the mould has been completed, a channel can be cut away in the plaster of each half immediately next to the impression made by the modelled leg, using a round modelling tool. This also creates a sharp edge to the depression in the mould. This operation must be carried out with the utmost care to avoid any breakdown of the edge itself (Figure 7.10).

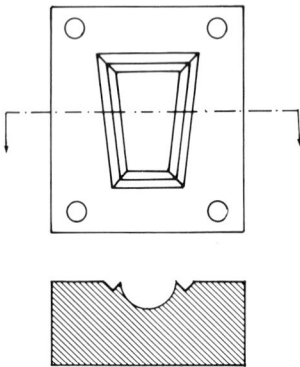

Figure 7.10. Press mould suitable for the making of a set of small tapered feet

To use the mould, press soft clay firmly into each half to form a perfect impression of the shape, leaving a little excess at the surface. Now press both parts of the mould firmly together. The two halves of clay will unite, allowing the surplus clay to be extruded into the surrounding channel where it is cut off by the sharp plaster edge.

Double casting

Only one surface of a cast is guaranteed smooth by a drain mould. The internal surface can be marred by raised draining ridges and, as have already been observed, problems associated with the maintenance of an even thickness.

This is of little importance where the inside is not readily visible, but the quality of the finished dish can be improved substantially by double casting. The perfect internal surface thus achieved is ideal for receiving decoration.

The initial stages for making a dish by double casting follow the same procedure as for the drain mould, but this is now used as a means of providing the first inner portion of the new mould. Thoroughly soap-size the whole upper surface and its edges, erect the casting box around it, seal, and pour in enough plaster to cover the existing surface by about 1¼ inches (30 mm). When the plaster has thoroughly set, remove the box and plunge the assembly into a bucket of water. This will make it possible to pull apart the old and new plaster sections. The drain mould is now known technically as the waste mould.

The newly-produced plaster will carry a hump in the form of the original clay model of the dish. A flat pancake of clay about ¼ inch (6 mm) thick is now rolled out (see page 78) and enough cut from it to cover the plaster hump. It must be carefully modelled so that the clay maintains an even thickness. A pencil line drawn on the plaster ¼ inch (6 mm) away from the base of the hump will serve as a guide and it may be necessary to cut away portions of the clay at certain points, such as the corners, to prevent the accumulation of unwanted clay. This clay surface will form the outer side of the mould, so it must be left perfectly true and smooth.

Consideration has now to be given to the foot which will obviously need to be smaller than the base of the dish itself. Another flat piece of clay is prepared about 1¼ inches (30 mm) in thickness and a piece cut from it of the same shape as the template. It must be tapered slightly on all sides to facilitate removal after casting, and then fixed down with slip to the clay already laid on the hump, lightly sealing the bottom edges with a modelling tool. Natch holes must be cut at the four corners of the first plaster pour and all visible plaster well soap-sized. The casting box can now be erected once more, sealed and plaster poured until it is just below the level of the foot piece. After setting, the two portions can be separated and all the applied clay removed. If the two portions of the mould are now linked, it will be seen that a cavity exists between them, equal to the required thickness of the dish (Figure 7.11).

After drying out, tie the two halves firmly together and pour casting slip into the mould in a continuous, steady stream. Tilting the mould a little, first to one side and then to the other during filling, aids an even spread of slip. Continue pouring until the well made by the added footpiece, is full. The mould is now left for twenty to twenty-five minutes to

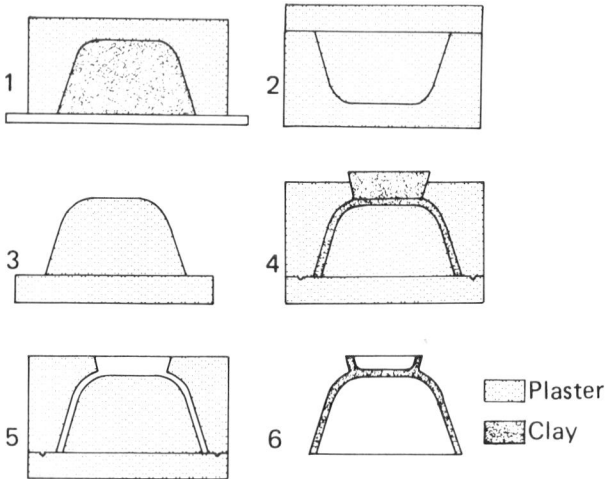

Figure 7.11. Stages in the double casting of the dish

allow sufficient time for clay to harden onto the sides of the mould which constitute the foot. Surplus slip can now be drained off leaving the clay foot adhering to the mould. The plaster will continue to dry the slip, and when the foot shows signs of coming away from the side, the top portion of the mould can be lifted off and the newly cast dish removed. The foot will be irregular but far too tall so it can be trimmed level at a desirable height with a sharp knife, guided by a conveniently sized block of wood.

Use and care of moulds

Any damage to the inside of a plaster of Paris mould ruins the quality of the cast made from it. It should never be sponged or scraped to remove adhering slip, which will peel away naturally once the plaster has fully dried again. Any dust inside a mould should be removed with a very soft brush. It is often necessary to discard the first cast from a new mould as it picks up odd specks of loose plaster, which, if fired in the clay, can cause a blow-out.

8

Hand-built pots

Excellent pots can be fashioned without the use of a potter's wheel by using slabs of clay of uniform thickness. These are best formed by rolling out a quantity of clay, which has been roughly flattened by the palm of the hand, between two prepared wooden slats of the same thickness (Figure 8.1). The rolling must be done on a surface to which the clay will

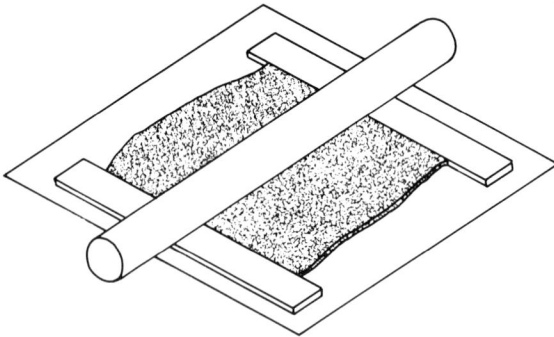

Figure 8.1. Rolling out clay slabs using slats and a wooden roller

not stick. Disused cartridge or wrapping papers are ideal, but newspaper is to be avoided since it is far too soft and the surface rapidly becomes torn causing innumerable pieces to roll into the clay. If the clay is particularly damp, it may be found to stick to the roller. This can be prevented by dusting it with a little fine grog.

Interesting variations in surface texture can be achieved by rolling the clay on such materials as hessian or corrugated paper. Once familiar with this technique, the student will instinctively take note of potential surfaces with which to experiment, as they come to hand.

Using formers

The former can be any object around which it is possible to model a flat layer of clay, but like the mould, it must be of suitable shape to allow for subsequent separation. Blocks of wood, with the corners slightly rounded, cardboard drums and cartons filled with plaster of Paris can all be used.

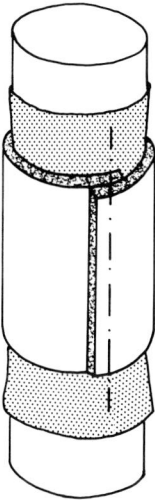

Figure 8.2. Method by which a true-fitting joint can be made when wrapping a former with clay

First cover the former with one or two layers of newspaper which must be made fast with a little adhesive. Next roll out a slab of clay of sufficient size to cover the mould. Cut this roughly to size and wrap it around the newspaper allowing it to overlap at the join. Now make a knife cut through both layers of clay at the point of overlap to guarantee perfect alignment of the two edges and allow the two waste strips of clay to be removed (Figure 8.2).

The two edges must then be lifted up, painted with slip, and modelled together. Surplus clay at the outer ends must also be trimmed. The former will slide out easily from one end or the other, depending on taper, but parallel sides present no difficulty. The formed clay is now stood on end on a suitable board in order to avoid distortion whilst the clay is drying to a leather-hard state. More often than not, the sheet of newspaper remains inside the clay and this serves as an ideal support during drying and can subsequently be removed. A problem can arise at the point of junction if the clay slab is textured since luting can destroy the textural pattern. Some potters make a feature of an irregular overlap but an alternative solution is to smooth a regular strip at the joint area and to border it with a deliberate line (Figure 8.3).

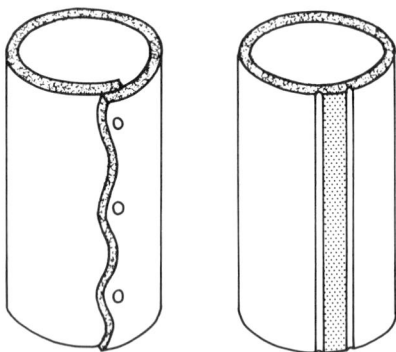

Figure 8.3. Suggestions for effecting a satisfactory overlap when using a textured clay slab on a former

When leather-hard, it is prudent to lute the joint on the inside as well before cutting out and fixing a base. If needed, lids and feet can be added. Useful formers can be made by casting blocks of plaster, cutting them to the desired shape with a hacksaw and steel scraper, finishing them with abrasive paper.

Plaster moulds used as formers

A drain mould, such as that described above, can also be used as an internal former. A slab of clay is rolled out and pressed into it.

Heavy pressure with the fingers should be avoided. The ideal tool for the purpose is a rubber kidney palette, but a reasonably dry soft sponge will do almost as well. After pressing, the top edge of clay must be trimmed level with the plaster. A final wipe of the clay with a damp sponge will leave an acceptable surface. After drying sufficiently, the dish can be lifted out.

Hump moulds

The same drain mould, in its capacity as a waste mould, can be used in yet another way but it is first necessary to make an accessory in the form of a stout plaster cylinder. To do this, stand a portion of large-diameter cardboard tube in a lump of clay, seal it round and fill with plaster. When this has set, the cardboard can be peeled off. Next, thoroughly soap-size the inside of the drain mould together with the top surface and accurately fill it with poured plaster. Before the plaster has set, one end of the previously made cylinder must be immersed into it at its centre, great care being taken to prevent the cylinder from touching the bottom of the mould. It must be held in this position until the plaster has just set and the cylinder is firmly united with the mould. As soon as this has occurred, it is advisable to reinforce the junction between mould and cylinder with a strong web of plaster. Surplus plaster, left over from the pour, is usually available for the purpose and an old knife serves well as a trowel (Figure 8.4).

When fully hardened, the newly poured plaster can be separated from the waste mould, together with the attached cylindrical handle, after a soak in water. If the dish is not very shallow and has fairly steep sides, separation can be helped by lining the waste mould with a thin layer of clay to take up the expansion of the plaster when poured. The waste portion can always be broken away if separation proves difficult.

The reinforcing plaster will prove its worth during the pulling action, which separation will demand. The newly-cast mould will have the appearance of a mushroom and is usually described as a hump or flop-over mould, though it is technically a former. It is helpful, when using a mould of this type, to enlist the services of an assistant to hold it upright with the end of the cylindrical handle resting on the table.

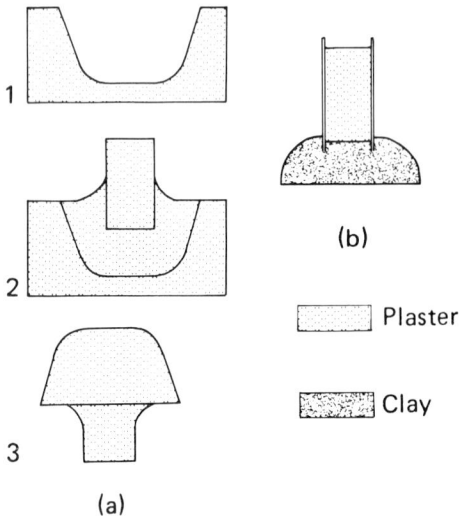

Figure 8.4. (a) Steps in the production of a flop-over (hump) mould. (b) A simple way of casting the plaster handle

The clay slab is rolled as before to a thickness of about ¼ inch (6 mm), picked up with both hands, lifted about 12 inches (300 mm) immediately above the mould and decisively dropped over the plaster (Figure 8.5). This action encourages the clay to assume the shape of the former. It will usually be necessary to complete the shaping by holding the mould up to eye level and patting and modelling as required. Once satisfactorily formed, the clay is trimmed around the base of the hump with a sharp knife and the whole put aside to dry

Figure 8.5. Rolled-out clay being 'flopped' over the hump mould

until the clay has 'frozen' to shape, at which stage it can be lifted free of the former.

Rolling out the clay on a supple cloth material can make handling easier. Being flexible, it can remain on the clay during flopping and help prevent marks forming during final hand-modelling. When eventually peeled off it leaves a pleasant texture.

Assembly from pieces

Pots with flat surfaces can be built up using cut-to-size pieces of slab clay in much the same way that a box is made by nailing together wooden slats. The required sizes must first be plotted on full-size card templates, due regard being given to clay thickness. If, for example, a square pot is envisaged, two sides will need to be wider than the others by twice the thickness of the slab. The base of any shaped pot must be large enough to incorporate the thickness of all the sides. When making triangular or more complex shapes it is often better to cut the templates to actual size and to mitre-trim the edges before assembly (Figure 8.6).

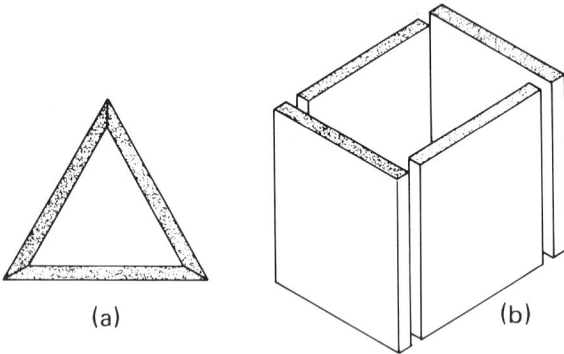

Figure 8.6. Slab ware. (a) Mitring the corners. (b) Allowing for the thickness of clay when determining the effective length of components

Using the templates, cut pieces of rolled clay to size with a knife, and allow them to dry and stiffen a little before being joined, especially if you have decided to mitre the edges. The various sections are assembled by coating adjacent edges with slip and then pressing them firmly together. This must be followed by luting with a modelling tool and subsequent cleaning up (Figure 8.7).

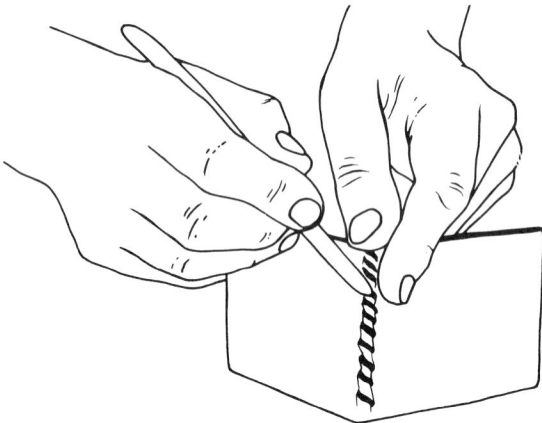

Figure 8.7. Luting the corner joints with a modelling tool

Whenever possible, the inside corners should be re-inforced by painting with a line of slip and adding a thin strip of rolled clay and modelling it to a pleasant curve. In addition to its reinforcing role this makes cleaning easier (Figure 8.8). Possible warping of the straight walls can be minimised by luting on a thin strip of clay around the inside top edge.

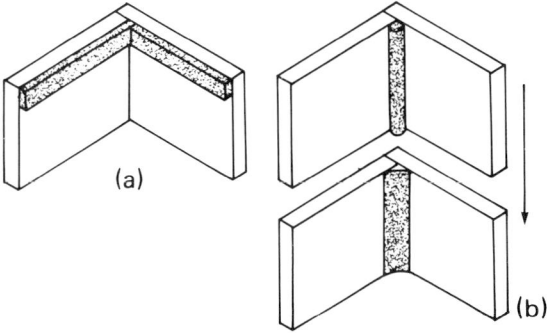

Figure 8.8. Reinforcing slab-built ware by: (a) Modelling on thin strips to minimise warping. (b) Modelling clay rolls into the corners

Lids for containers of this type can be made by using two rather thinner clay slabs pressed together with slip, one of the overall size of the container, or slightly larger if an overhang is required, and the other to fit freely inside. To ensure a good fit, both pot and lid must be made at the same time and due allowance made for subsequent layers of glaze.

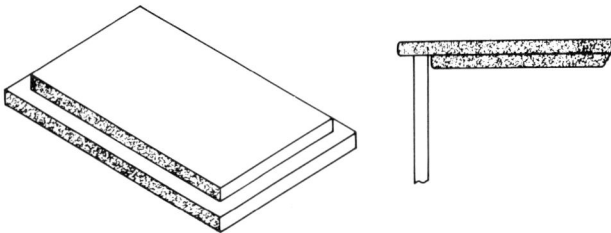

Figure 8.9. Slab lids

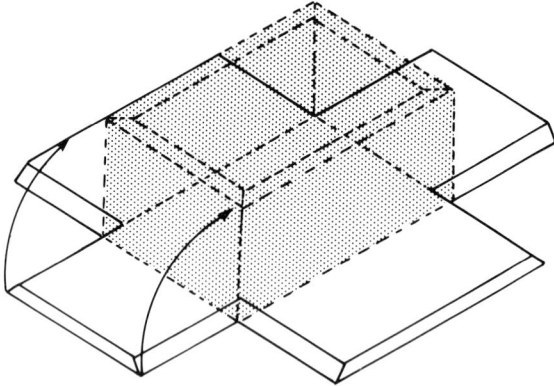

Figure 8.10. Raising walls from a clay development

The knob can also be made of clay. An interesting variation, providing a contrast of materials, can be made by piercing two holes in the lid at specific points through which a hardwood knob can eventually be screwed (Figure 8.9).

Small regular-shaped pots can be raised from a single slab. This entails the construction of a card template. Procedure is much as before and the jointing edges mitred, but in this case bending up of the sides is best done before the clay stiffens. It is helpful to raise the sides against a piece of wood held along the line of the base (Figure 8.10).

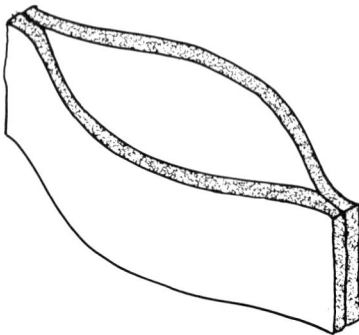

Figure 8.11. Free-shaped pot with pinched joints

Joints must be brushed with slip, luted, and the pot then set aside to stiffen prior to final shaping and cleaning up. To aid this process, it is helpful to rest the sides, in turns, on a flat surface and to smooth the inside with a flat piece of wood such as a ruler. Free-shaped pots are another possibility, the ends of the clay slabs being overlapped and squeezed together whilst still plastic to make a design feature (Figure 8.11).

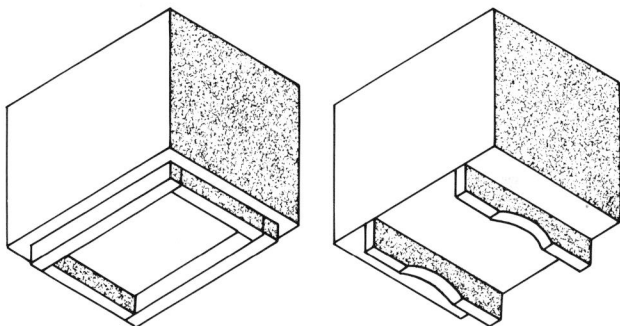

Figure 8.12. Slab-built pieces viewed from beneath to illustrate two alternative methods of providing foot support

If it is considered appropriate to raise a slab-built pot on some kind of foot, small pieces of shaped slab or a plinth made up in the form of a smaller shallow box without a base, can be modelled on (Figure 8.12).

Pots made with layers of clay

Decorative vases can be made by cutting out hollowed clay shapes from rolled out slabs and joining them one on top of the other with slip. A template will ensure uniformity of shape, though it can prove interesting to combine differing shapes and sizes in the same composition.

Biscuit cutters can be used for cutting out centres and even for the outside if a round pot is being made. Some of these cutters have ribbed edges which can create an interesting texture (Figure 8.13). Joints between the layers must be well luted on the inside as work proceeds.

This style of slab work is similar to the building up of pots by the gradual addition of successive layers of clay to the walls. Native African potters, often the women of a tribe, make beautiful, large water and cooking pots which are so regular and well-built that they appear to have been finished with the aid of a wheel. These potters add extra clay by extruding it through the finger and thumb in similar manner

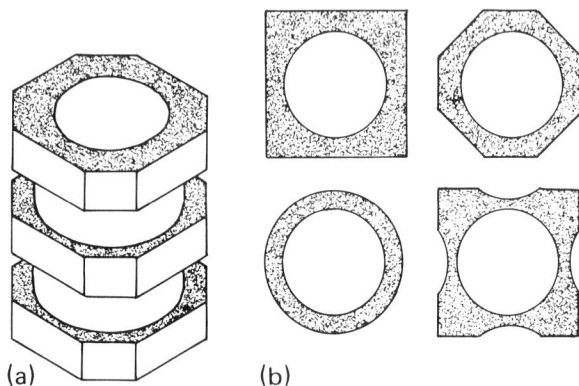

Figure 8.13. Building pots in layers. (a) Adding interest by alternating shapes. (b) Suggestions for shapes of further layers

to that employed by a professional glazier laying putty. They then consolidate it to the required shape between the palm of the hand and a wooden paddle. It is a skill which needs much practice to perfect.

A similar method, suitable for a beginner, is known as coiling. A base of required shape and size is cut from a slab of clay and the walls built up on it by adding successive rolls of clay. It is a good practice to keep the clay 'open' by kneading some fine grog into it before use when making a coiled pot, especially if it is a large one.

Preparing rolls of clay

It is not as easy as it would appear to produce an even roll of clay. All too often, the circular cross section becomes first oval, and then progressively flatter and more uneven. It is also liable to become very thin at one end and break. The clay should be soft but not sticky. As in slab making, it is best rolled on a large piece of paper. Begin with a roughly modelled thick roll of clay then thin it by moving backwards and forwards across the paper with the outstretched fingers held parallel with the roll and moving simultaneously from the centre to the outer ends. To preserve a perfect round cross-section the roll must be moved through a distance equal to its circumference so that each part receives equal hand pressure (Figure 8.14).

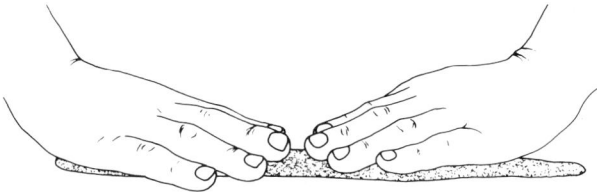

Figure 8.14. Correct hand position when making clay rolls

If the roll becomes too long to handle before being sufficiently thin, it should be cut into halves and each rolled individually to the correct diameter. Alternatively, wad boxes are available which extrude clay through a die on the grease-gun principle. It is best to prepare a stock of rolls before commencing to build a pot. They can be stored in a plastic bag to prevent them from drying out. Rolls about ½ inch (12 mm) in diameter are a good size with which to start.

Building a coiled pot

It is helpful to prepare full-size templates of the side profile and base of the proposed pot. Using the template as a guide, cut the base from a slab of clay and place on a piece of flat blockboard or tile. There are two methods of building the walls – either using a long roll round and round until it is used up, or cutting off a new roll for each layer. The beginner will find the latter method easier to control and it will give a more even top.

The first roll is laid carefully onto the shaped base and well modelled to it both inside and out. The ends of the roll should be spliced where they meet to keep the top level. Successive rolls are then built up, one upon the other, each in turn well modelled to its predecessor.

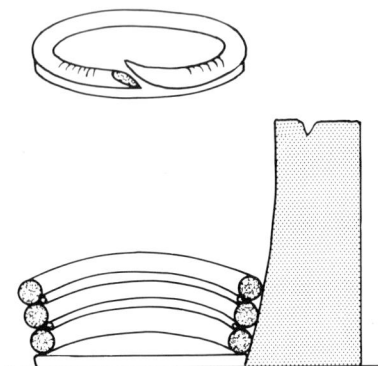

Figure 8.15. Building a coiled pot. (a) Splicing the ends of each coil. (b) Using the template to check the shape

The outside of the pot can either be left to display the basic shape of the coils or smoothed to give a more normal clay surface. The latter will make for a stronger wall. In either case luting must be carried out on the inside to prevent the rolls from separating during firing. It is sometimes necessary to add thin subsidiary clay rolls in the spaces between the coils to make a perfectly smooth surface. Straight-sided pots are made by laying on the coils immediately above one another. Shaping is achieved by allowing each newly added roll to slightly overlap the previous one. This is where the side template can prove tremendously helpful (Figure 8.15).

Plate 1. Composite pieces decorated with clay stamps. The small pot is an example of glaze decoration

Plate 2. Bottle jug decorated with paper resist. The vases and small bowl illustrate the value of tin glaze in decoration

Plate 3. The casserole and jug are sprig decorated. The bowl is an example of filled inlay

Plate 4. A marbled bowl, feathered dishes and a vase in agate ware

Plate 5. Vase decorated with brushwork on a matt glaze. The junket bowls were painted in under-glaze colours

Plate 6. Three pieces built up on formers from clay rolled out on a textured surface. The thrown bowl has been shaped by cutting the upper edge

Plate 7. Three pieces illustrating pierced decoration

Plate 8. The two bowls in the background illustrate the sgraffito technique. The bowl in the foreground shows the use of slip trailing

A limited number of rolls can be added at one sitting since after a while the soft clay will tend to sag. When signs of this are evident, the pot should be set aside for a day or so to harden before the next layers are added. This procedure may need to be repeated over several days if a tall pot is being made. Care must be taken to finish the top of a coiled pot, possibly by developing an outward flare or an interestingly modelled rim. Coiled pots can easily look as if they are not really finished. The technique of coiling means that pots can be made which are not of the usual basic round shape, for instance, they can be asymmetric or spirally formed and, theoretically, can be of limitless size. It is not as easy as it appears to control coiling, but it affords excellent practice in the handling of clay and provides a useful skill if the student should wish to embark on pottery sculpture.

Pinched pots

This is a simple method of modelling which relies purely on the action of the fingers and thumbs. It is usually limited to the making of small objects, though there is no reason why more ambitious pots cannot be undertaken by assembling pinched units. Success relies in establishing a good rhythm of work.

To make a pinched pot take a ball of soft clay and lightly flatten it at both top and bottom. Place this on a piece of thick paper, slightly larger than the ball itself. Then fold the fingers of both hands around the clay with the two thumbs meeting at the top centre. Make a depression into the clay with one thumb, similar to that made during the initial throwing of a pot on the wheel. Now place both thumbs within the formed cavity allowing the fingers to rest comfortably over the top rim. The finger tips on the outside and thumbs inside must exactly oppose one another. Holding the pot in this way move the pot through a quarter circle to the right or left (whichever direction is adopted must be maintained throughout), at the same time squeezing the clay very gently between the fingers and thumbs. Return the hands to their original position and make another quarter turn.

This rhythm is repeated and maintained, moving the fingers up or down the clay wall as appropriate. Regularity of movement will make for an even pot. It is a good idea to thin from the bottom upwards since a thick top will reduce undue spreading (Figure 8.16).

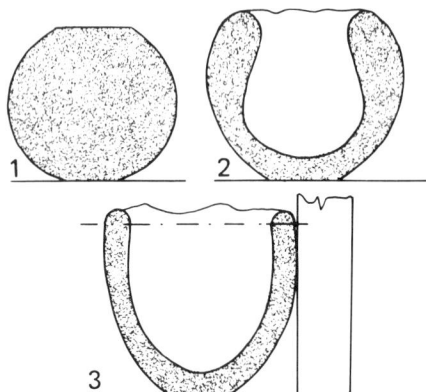

Figure 8.16. Steps in the making of a pinched pot

As in throwing, shape can be controlled by variation in pressure between the inside thumb and the fingers on the outside. It cannot be too strongly emphasised that pressure must be very lightly applied if the shape is to be controlled. Should the clay tend to become dry and brittle as a result of being worked by hot hands, they should be dampened before resuming work. The finished pot will bear finger marks which are a feature of the work and should not be removed. However it may be desirable to level the top. This can be achieved by making a series of marks from a template which coincides with the lowest point and trimming away the waste with a knife. The edge should subsequently be rounded.

Composite forms

Exciting pots can be made by combining the various methods which have been outlined. Slab-built sections can, for example, be surmounted by coiled or thrown tops. Shapes

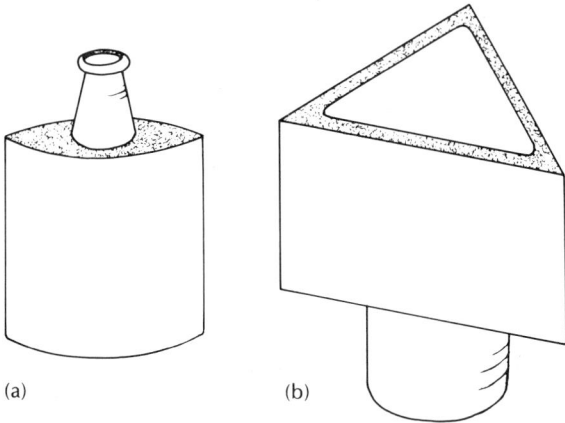

Figure 8.17. Examples of composite forms. (a) Oval body built up on a former with added thrown neck. (b) Slab-built triangular body added to a thrown plinth

made on formers can be incorporated into thrown shapes – the possibilities are endless (Figure 8.17). Thrown shapes, too, can be cut and remodelled to form units in a composition.

9

Ceramic decoration

The complexity of pottery as a craft is well demonstrated by the wealth of decorative techniques associated with it. Decoration can be applied to a pot at every stage of its making, irrespective of the manner in which it is formed. With such a range of possibilities for embellishment, the student must guard against the temptation to apply decoration for its own sake or to use it to cover defects in making. The application of a beautiful glaze is sometimes all that is needed to complement a truly graceful pot. Decoration must never be laboured and the great art in decorating is to know just when to stop. This skill can only be cultivated by studying the work of experts in the field, by personal experience and by increased dexterity in application.

Decoration applied during making

Impressions in plastic clay
One method, the rolling out of clay on a textured surface, was described on page 179. Clay decoration of a more specific kind can be applied whilst the clay is still plastic and before it is cut to size, by making impressions in it either with some form of stamp or by using an embossed roller. Any common object of suitable size can be used as a stamp – a toothed wheel from an old clock, a piece of dowel rod, a decorative plastic bottle cap, the open end of a test tube to name just a few possibilities. When many of these objects are used it is useful to mount them on the end of a small piece of wood for ease of handling. A more deliberate stamp can be

made by filing motifs into the end of a piece of close-grained hardwood, or by casting it in plaster of Paris.

There are two methods by which these plaster stamps can be made. The direct method entails carving into the end of a small block of cast plaster before it has fully dried out. This is similar to the stick print. In the more indirect method the relief design is modelled as a raised unit on a block of clay. When complete, a small cottle about 3 inches (75 mm) high is erected around it. This can be of stiff card, generously overlapped and well stapled at the joint. It should be lightly pressed into the clay block to create a seal and a little extra clay modelled around the outside to prevent any leakage of the plaster. Plaster of slightly stronger mix than that used for mould-making is then poured in to fill the cottle. When set, the card is removed, together with the clay model, to reveal a plaster stamp bearing an impression exactly opposite to that which was modelled in clay.

A further possibility lies in modelling the complete stamp in clay and baking it in the next biscuit kiln. When a stamp is being used, care must be taken not to exert too heavy a pressure upon it as this will lead to unnecessary distortion and weakness in the clay. Uneven stamping must also be avoided. It is wise to restrict stamp decoration to areas away from edges of clay which will later be jointed so that the pattern is not marred by the luting which will be necessary when the parts are finally assembled (Figure 9.1)

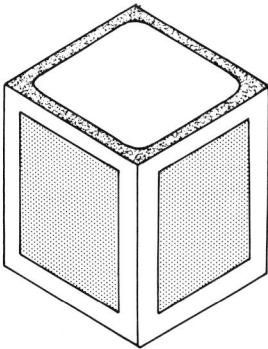

Figure 9.1. Pattern areas not marred by the luting

Repeat patterns can be pressed into clay using some form of roller. For large surfaces, the wooden roller used to produce slabs can be modified by glueing shaped units of felt or card to its surface with a waterproof glue such as 'Araldite' (Figure 9.2).

Figure 9.2.   Using a felt pattern roller

Smaller repeat patterns can be created using a roulette wheel which can be made in either plaster or clay. To make it in clay roll out a slab about $7/8$–1 inch (22–25 mm) thick and cut from it a circular piece about 3 inches (77 mm) in diameter. When this has dried to a leather-hard state turn it on the potter's wheel to make every surface absolutely true. Whilst it is still spinning on the wheel pierce a small hole at its centre to receive a thick wire for the handle. After removal from the wheel, divide the rim into an equal number of parts and either cut or apply with slip a regularly repeating motif as a relief unit in each section. The prepared disc is finally baked in the next biscuit kiln.

A similar procedure can be adopted if the roulette is to be made in plaster of Paris except that it must commence by casting a suitable disc on an accurately prepared base and the addition of relief units will be impossible.

Whether of biscuit or plaster, the roulette must be furnished with a suitably made thick wire handle which will make it possible for it to be rolled over the plastic clay and so leave a recessed or embossed pattern (Figure 9.3). A more sophisticated metal handle and axle could be made by a student with metalworking skills.

Basic patterns can also be added at this stage by preparing a cut-out in thick card and rolling it onto the clay. An impression of the card will remain after it has been lifted away. All these stamped-in patterns are enhanced by the glaze which will tend to flow into the deeper parts giving them a darker tone.

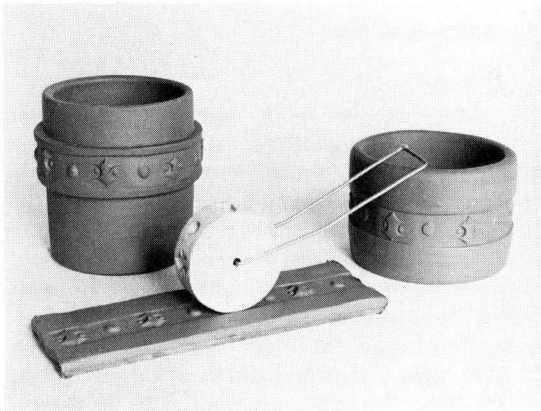

Figure 9.3. A biscuited roulette wheel and the end product

An interesting surface can be given to a thrown pot purely by creating ridges with the fingers or a suitably shaped modelling tool during making. Adequate support must be given to the inside of the pot by the left hand to offset the added pressure which is exerted from the outside by the tool.

Agate ware
This style of pottery possesses a 'built-in' all-over pattern inherent in the method of making. Two bodies of contrasting

97

colour are separately prepared for throwing and then lightly wedged together so that when cut, the surface displays a veined appearance. It is important for the two bodies to have a similar shrinkage coefficient. Alternatively, the same body can be used for each portion, except that one is coloured by the incorporation of a staining oxide. The pot is then thrown, using the combined clays, as rapidly as possible. Continual coning and depressing will tend to bring about too fine a mixture between the two. The full result of the process will not be readily visible until the pot has been turned when the outside will display a marbled appearance similar to that of agate stone from which the ware takes its name.

Cutting at the leather-hard stage

Modifying the shape
It is in this state that clay lends itself to more varied treatment. It can be handled without fear of distortion, it is not sticky, can be cut, joined, and worked. Alterations can be made to the outside shape, provided that the pot itself has been thrown with a wall of sufficient thickness. Interesting bowls can be made by dividing the circumference into a regular number of divisions and then cutting facets into each division with a thin, sharp knife. The facetted sides are highlighted by the contrast they make with the round inside and, if the bowl tapers sharply towards the foot, by the circularity of the base. The same treatment could be given to the central portion of a taller pot. To look good, the facets must be cut regularly and the angle of cut checked against a tri- or bevel square or a card template of the required profile (Figure 9.4).

The need to divide the circumference of a pot into a number of equal divisions frequently occurs when decoration has to be applied. The easiest way is to cut a long strip of paper (such as the edge of a newspaper) about ⅜ inch (10 mm) wide and to wrap it around the top of the pot.

Cut this to length at the meeting point to produce a paper strip which exactly represents the circumference of the pot. This strip can then be folded as many times as necessary to form the number of required spaces. If the strip is now returned to the original position the crease points can be transferred to the clay. Division of the outside of a pot into equal areas can be achieved by resting a square on the table and lining it up to coincide with the circumference points

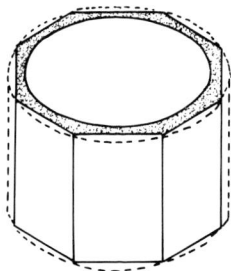

Figure 9.4. Modifying basic shape by the cutting of facets

already registered. A modelling tool or pencil held at right-angles to the square can now be used to trace a vertical line which passes through the required point.

Fluting

The ability to create equal spaces and to draw vertical lines on a pot is nowhere more useful than in the process of fluting where vertical grooves are cut regularly into the clay surface. It is quite disastrous to cut flutes around the surface only to find that there is just too much, or not enough, space left for the last one. The same arrangement with the square can be adopted to work an initial small channel with a modelling tool drawn down gradually from the top to the bottom of the pot. If this is repeated several times an appreciable groove will result. Each flute is worked in the same way. These preliminary grooves will prove invaluable in keeping the line of the flute even during the widening and deepening which follows as the true contour is worked. A coiling tool is useful for this job or a home-made tool can be made from a piece of old clock spring as described for the making of a turning tool on page 6. As in so many pottery operations, the natural

Figure 9.5. An example of the use of fluting in a vase

curve of the forefinger provides an excellent finishing tool if moistened with a little water (Figure 9.5).

Flutes can either be spaced or cut adjacent to one another to form a series of meeting edges.

Modifying the profile
The character of a basic thrown shape can be completely changed by carving the upper rim to create a new, and not necessarily regular, profile (Figure 9.6).

Forms of inlay
Intricate decoration can be cut into leather-hard clay by incising lines with either a modelling tool, a bent wire or a blunt-pointed awl. The choice of tool influences the strength

of line, thus allowing for varied composition. The design can be lightly sketched onto the clay as a guide. Any flaking at the edges of the incised line should be dusted away with a soft brush. These incised lines will be emphasised by the glaze which will run into the small channels and present a darker appearance.

The pattern can be made to stand out more sharply by filling the incised lines with a slip of contrasting clay or one which has been stained with a metal-colouring pigment. Merely painting the small groove with an underglaze colour or a pigment solution is all that is sometimes needed. The

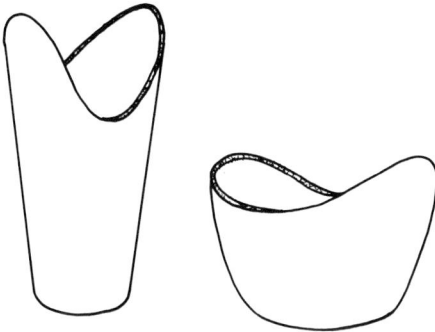

Figure 9.6.   Altering the pot profile by cutting the rim

parent surface will in all cases need cleaning when thoroughly dry to give a clean edge to the coloured line. This must be carried out using some form of scraper. A wet sponge would, of course, defeat its own object.

The technique can be taken one stage further. Units of pattern can be carried into the clay by first making vertical cuts no more than ⅛ inch (4 mm) deep around the edges of the pattern and removing the waste by working up to them with lino tools. The base of the recess should be levelled to the same ⅛ inch (4 mm) depth, painted with slip and the clay which is to be inlaid pressed in, a little at a time, to avoid trapping any air. This clay filler should not be too wet and should match, as nearly as possible, the state of dryness of the pot itself. The surface is scraped level when the clays have dried sufficiently to avoid blurring. This is an inlay technique similar to that used for making encaustic tiles; see page 123.

Adding cut-out clay shapes
An attractive decoration can be provided by adding cut-out clay shapes with slip. Much can be made of the luting process allowing regular pressing with a modelling tool to produce a decorative edge. Rolls of clay applied in the same manner can form interesting strips of vertical decoration (Figure 9.7).

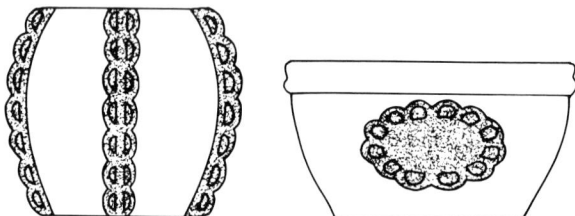

Figure 9.7. Simple decoration using added clay decoratively pressed on with a modelling tool

Slabs of clay already impressed with a stamp decoration can be cut to shape and fixed with slip to a turned pot either as bands of pattern or as individual pieces. More sophisticated applied ornament can be added in the form of sprigs. This is the method employed in the production of traditional Wedgwood ware.

Sprigging
The motif must be designed so that each of its facets is an integral part of the whole forming a kind of medallion. It is first modelled on a perfectly flat piece of clay. This can be roughed out by cutting the main shapes from thinly rolled clay and sticking them with slip in their relevant positions on the flat clay. These are allowed to harden and then the final carving and modelling of the design can be completed. All

102

edges must be given a top-tapering curve and a thorough check made to ensure that no section presents any undercuts.

The flat clay on which the unit has been modelled is now cleanly cut to a size about ¾ inch (19 mm) larger all around than the motif itself. Erect a clay wall around the motif, seal and pour in the plaster. When the plaster has set remove both the clay wall and the modelled motif. The sprig mould which has been cast is now allowed to dry thoroughly, its flatness checked by gently rubbing the surface on a sheet of fine glasspaper, and any resulting dust removed with a soft brush. To use the sprig mould, press clay of the same, or a contrasting, colour firmly into it with both thumbs, making sure that every recess is adequately filled. Remove surplus clay with a flat scraper or the side of a palette knife blade until the clay filling is flush with the flat plaster surface. Care must be taken to avoid undue scraping of the accurate plaster surface.

Leave the clay for a moment or so, after which it should be possible to lift the clay relief, known as the sprig, from the plaster. It will be quite delicate and the lifting is best carried out with the aid of a dab of damp clay used as a suction pad (Figure 9.8).

Before fixing to the pot, the back of the sprig must be given a thin coating of slip and the pot surface dampened with a sponge. Sprigs need careful handling and every effort must be made to prevent distortion of the modelled surface. The first very light pressure should be at the centre, then work gradually towards the outside edges to ensure that no air is trapped between the surfaces of the sprig and the pot. Any cleaning up of the contact edges is best delayed until the slip has thoroughly dried, especially if it has been made in a contrasting colour.

Any residual clay from the initial levelling in the mould should be discarded since it will most probably be contaminated with plaster scrapings. Sprigs used on a pot with a very sharply curved surface are liable, when laid, to crack at the centre. This can be avoided by modelling the initial master relief on a similarly curved surface so that every sprig will then leave the mould pre-shaped to the correct curvature.

In some situations, a larger sprig can be applied directly to the inside of a newly thrown bowl which is still resting on the wheel. The mould is filled with clay and levelled in the usual

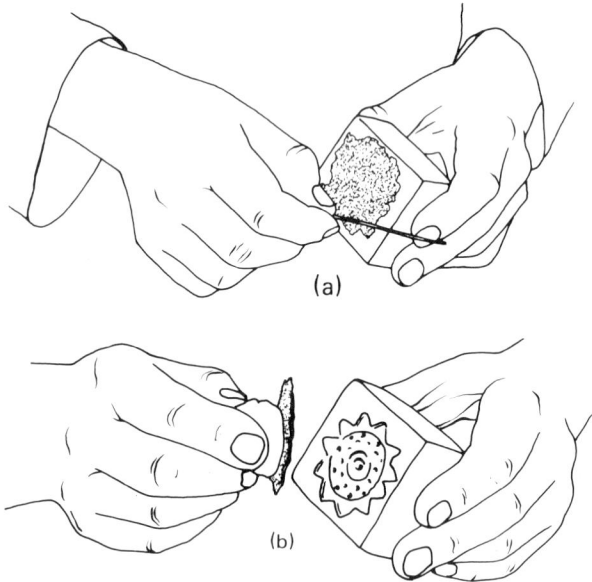

Figure 9.8. Producing a sprig from the mould. (a) Levelling the surface with a palette knife. (b) Lifting the sprig free by clay suction

way, but the sprig is not removed. Instead, the filled mould is pressed directly into the wet clay, causing the sprig to become attached to it, and the mould lifted free.

Piercing
Since leather-hard clay can easily be cut with a sharp knife, patterns can be pierced in the clay wall of a pot or its lid. Such decoration can fulfil a utilitarian as well as a decorative role. A ceramic container for a child's night-light, a lamp fitted with

an internal bulb, and the lid of a pot-pourri jar, are all examples of this. The required shapes can be cut out in newspaper, dampened, and moulded to the clay surface. A line can then be drawn around them with a pencil or a scriber. It is not good practice to make a direct cut along the plotted line since this can cause local cracking. An initial hole should first be cut at the centre of each shape and the remaining waste cut away by a gradual paring back to the line with a small knife such as a penknife. Webs between the pierced portions must be of sufficient width to retain adequate strength in the basic clay wall. The hard cut edges can be softened with a damp sponge or brush. Piercing and applied relief can often be combined to good effect if a pierced shape is reflected by a similar one added as relief near to it.

Slip ware

As the name implies, all styles of slip ware decoration rely on the application of natural clay slip as opposed to the deflocculated variety used for casting. It should be well sieved and free-flowing, like a batter. Slips can be of natural clay colour – white or brown – or they may be stained with colouring oxides. White slip forms the basis for most colours. A small portion of the oxide is ground with a little slip, either in a pestle and mortar, or with a palette knife on a piece of thick glass, before being returned and stirred into the main bulk of slip. The complete mixture is then sieved to encourage a homogeneous mix. Body stains are also available from suppliers. These are often listed as universal stains, since they can also be used to colour glazes. Black slip is easily made by adding manganese dioxide to one of brown earthenware.

Decoration can be applied using prepared slip as a paint but it does not flow well from a brush which cannot retain a sufficient charge to complete a full stroke. Areas of slip can, however, be painted onto a leather-hard pot as a contrasting ground for subsequent pattern work.

Sgraffito

The technique takes its name from an Italian word 'sgraffire' meaning 'to scratch'. The areas of the pot to be decorated are first dampened with a sponge to create a good bond and then covered with a good layer of contrasting slip, either by painting with a large soft brush, by pouring, or by dipping. When this layer has hardened a little, the proposed design is scratched or cut through it using a modelling tool of either wood or steel, a scriber or a small penknife blade, to reveal the colour of the clay beneath. A wide variation is possible, from the scratching of a fine line to the removal of large design areas. The clay removed should be dusted clear with a soft brush. It is important to work on the slip at its optimum state of dryness; if it is too dry the edges of a scratched line will chip.

The pre-designed pattern can be drawn lightly in pencil on the slipped surface as a guide for working. A very much bolder and more direct pattern can be made simply by drawing into the still-wet slip with a finger tip or a comb cut from stout cardboard, in a similar fashion to that adopted in the making of paste-combed paper.

This style of decoration can be applied to any part of a pot but is particularly useful as a means of embellishing the inside of a bowl, producing decorative bands and for creating interesting little 'windows' on small articles such as mugs or jugs.

Trailing

Complete patterns can be laid down using a slip trailer in the same way as a confectioner decorates a cake from an icing bag. The skill was widely practised by seventeenth century potters such as Thomas Toft, whose masterpieces included large trailed plates and dishes.

Several types of trailer are on the market. The rubber flattened balloon type, in which a glass nozzle can be inserted, is the best sort (Figure 9.9). This permits well-controlled squeezing by the fingers against the palm of the hand and, by using a series of interchangeable nozzles of differing bore, variations in the strength of the trailed line are

106

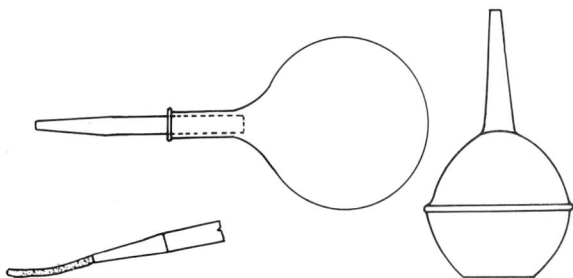

Figure 9.9. Two types of trailer

possible. The art of trailing lies in preventing the nozzle from making direct contact with the clay ground, so allowing the extruded slip to fall cleanly onto the surface (Figure 9.10).

This results in a round-sectioned trail which is highlighted by the play of light and shadow upon it. The beginner is advised to practise trailing on a Formica sheet or similar surface before attempting the technique on the more difficult curving surface of a pot. The fact that an incorrectly

Figure 9.10. Using a trailer

107

applied piece of trailing can be sponged off and repeated should give confidence.

The trailer can be filled with slip using a plastic syringe. Slip must be slowly sucked into the syringe with its aperture dipped well into the stock mixture to prevent drawing in unwanted air. Once filled and the nozzle fitted the bag should also be lightly squeezed to remove any air within it. There is nothing more frustrating than to see a well trailed pattern ruined by a sudden splash of slip resulting from a trapped air bubble.

Marbling

This is a slipware technique usually applied to the insides of bowls and dishes or flat surfaces. The inside of the leather-hard bowl is coated with a layer of wet slip used as a glaze. A small quantity, sufficient to cover the surface, is poured into the bowl which is then tilted and turned so that the slip is swilled over the whole area, any surplus being allowed to drain away over the edge. No attempt must ever be made to touch up this poured slip surface. A contrasting slip of an exactly similar consistency is then dribbled from the side into the wet layer and swirled into it by further dexterous turning of the bowl.

The art can only be acquired through practice and it is impossible to give precise instructions since the behaviour of the various slips varies considerably. The contrasting swirl lines can be followed and tilting directed so as to encourage them to move along graceful rhythmic paths. Part of the attraction of this type of pattern is its spontaneity and individuality. If possible, the final swirl should be towards the edge of the bowl so that it can drain out neatly at the rim. Over-shaking or too vigorous an attempt to marble can lead to an indiscriminate mixing of the two slips and an indeterminate pattern. Flooding the semi-dry bowl with wet slip will inevitably soften it, so the marbling procedure must be carried out as quickly as possible. It helps if the bowl can be supported inside another of suitable contour during drying. If it has been formed in a plaster mould, this will provide the ideal support.

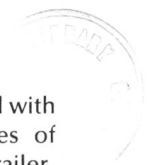

Feathering

For this method of decoration, the clay surface is coated with wet slip in the same manner as for marbling. Lines of contrasting coloured slip are then laid across it from a trailer, or if the pot can be spun on a wheel, in concentric rings. Great care must be taken to prevent the trailer nozzle from fouling the wet slip. A small well-pointed camel hair brush, a bristle or, as was traditionally used, a feather, is then very lightly drawn through the trailed lines, merely tickling their surface. Added stability and control can be given to the brush by holding it with clenched fist of the other. Too heavy a pressure on the brush will forge unsightly channels in the slipped background. The feathering action will drag a small portion of each trailed line along with it and modify it into the form of a double ogee. Similar strokes are made across or

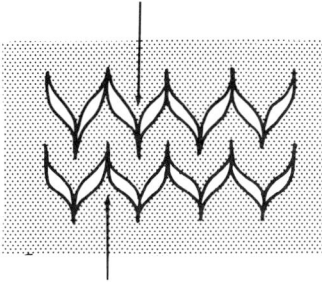

Figure 9.11. The double-ogee effect produced by feathering

around the whole surface at regular intervals of about ¾–⅝ inch (19–15 mm). A further series of feathered lines can be made in the spaces between those originally drawn, working in the opposite direction (Figure 9.11).

If applied to concentric lines of trailing, feathering is, of course, practised radially.

Fern patterns

Interesting and novel little units of decoration can be developed by using a technique discovered by the early slipware potters. A small quantity of a colouring agent, such as cobalt oxide, is ground in a mortar with a little tobacco – one cigarette with the paper removed is quite sufficient – and water, and then sieved through a 120 mesh lawn. Blobs of this liquid are now dropped onto an area of wet slip where they will gradually seep into it to form a leaf-like pattern. It is not, of course, possible to exercise complete control over the ultimate result but distribution of the active liquid can be a deliberate one. It can be allowed to drain in a line and the blobs can either be placed in predetermined positions, or sprinkled haphazardly.

Direct application of colour

Leather-hard clay can be decorated with brushwork using underglaze colours or metallic colouring oxides. These colours are mixed with a little water and ground well on a glass slab with a palette knife (Figure 9.12).

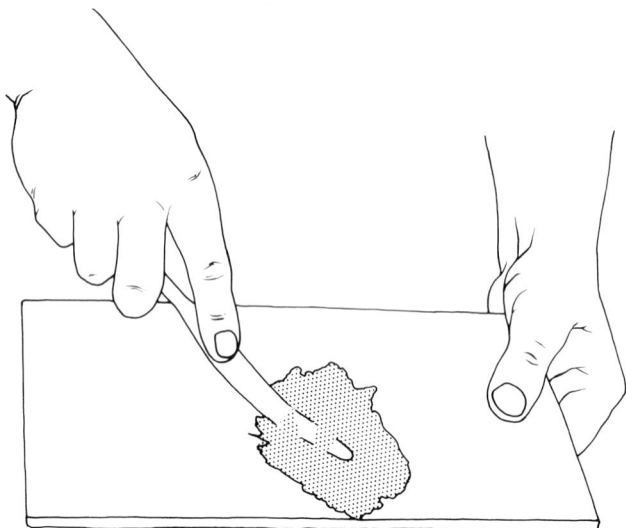

Figure 9.12. Grinding ceramic colours on a glass slab – note the bending of the palette knife to create the grinding action

The colours are burnt into the clay during the biscuit fire and are thus made safe from running during the application of a glaze. As will be seen later, underglaze colours are also painted on biscuited clay but it is far easier to paint on the green clay and there is an added bonus in that mistakes can easily be rectified. Yellows and reds, however, are not really suitable for application on raw clay since they tend to burn away completely.

Resist method

If a bold cut-out pattern is called for, newspaper, which moulds to any complex shape when dampened with water, will serve as an excellent resist material. Pattern areas can be cut from the newspaper, soaked briefly in water and applied to the clay surface by patting gently with a damp sponge. The colour mixture can then be painted or spun over the whole area. When this has dried sufficiently the newspaper can be peeled off gently. Alternatively, the surface may be sprayed with colour, using a simple spray diffuser or a spatter brush. With this method a gradation of colour is made possible.

This resist technique is applicable to coloured slip as well as to underglaze colours. Obviously thought must be given to the selection of contrasting colour areas. It is pointless, for example, to spray cobalt or iron oxide onto the inside of a brown earthenware bowl. It would be far better to spin a layer of white slip over the surface before applying the design.

All decoration applied at the raw-clay stage must be given a transparent glaze, which, if applied over multi-coloured brushwork, must also be clear. If the same clear glaze is used over sgraffito, marbling, trailing, and feathering, the resultant contrast will be that of the natural clays. A coloured transparent glaze, on the other hand, will produce contrast in the form of two tones of the same colour. For example a copper-stained glaze would render any white slip a light green and impart a much darker green to the clay of the basic pot. This can have a unifying effect which is very pleasant.

Scope for originality

Much of the fun of decorating pottery results from the multitude of ways in which the various decorative techniques can be combined. Larger areas, for example, can be masked with the newspaper resist and subsequently given an underglaze brush motif, or receive an applied sprig. Fluted sections can be incorporated in thrown pots or motifs trailed on facetted planes. There is ample scope for imaginative experimentation, always bearing in mind that simplicity of design is often the most effective.

Decoration at the biscuit stage

Underglaze colours
Although these are often used on green clay, they are more closely associated with the decoration of biscuit ware. The colours are prepared in the same manner, but in order to prevent then from being disturbed by glazing, a few drops of gum-arabic must also be ground into the mixture on the glass plate. If too much is added, the painting will become resistant to the glaze. Alternatively, the colours may be ground with a ready-prepared underglaze medium which is available from suppliers. Turpentine and fat oil too, are sometimes used as a medium to allow better control of the colours, but the pot must then be low-fired to about 700°C before it can be glazed in order to burn off the oil and this method is not to be recommended for an amateur potter.

Painting on porous biscuit will present a greater challenge than painting on the raw clay and any mistakes are virtually impossible to erase. Brush strokes must be made with a fully charged brush and be controlled extremely well. A laboriously painted area can appear streaky and patchy. The pattern must in every case be sealed with a clear glaze. The majority of underglaze colours are designed to withstand a fire of 1280°C, though some operate at a much lower temperature. Always check whether the maximum firing temperature of the colours and the glaze are compatible.

Colours can be mixed together, though not always with predictable results. Results vary with the colour of the biscuit upon which they are worked. Some colours tend to burn away and need fairly dense application whilst others are liable to deepen in colour on firing and must be used sparingly. It is a good idea for a beginner to paint, glaze and fire a test piece with a few specimen strokes of each colour on a slab of biscuit. This will provide valuable information concerning the tonal values and behaviour of the individual colours under varying glaze conditions.

Banding
This type of decoration is made by running rings of colour onto the pot. The bands are applied by centring the pot on a banding wheel, giving it a whirl, and holding the charged

Figure 9.13. Providing support when using the brush in banding

brush still, against it. It is vital that the hairs of the brush should be lined up away from the direction of rotation and that the hand should be well supported (Figure 9.13).

It is possible to buy special lining and banding brushes but an ordinary good quality camel hair brush will work quite well.

Underglaze crayons

These are used in the same manner as chalks, and the underglaze colours which they contain are deposited on the biscuit. They do not allow for fine detail and the biscuit surface needs to be as smooth as possible to minimise crayon 'bite' and the appearance of broken lines, but they do produce a distinctive pattern. After application any dust must be blown away prior to glazing. Underglaze felt-tipped pens, which allow a much more intricate style, are also obtainable.

Wax resist

The resist technique has already been introduced (see page 111) and is frequently applied to biscuit ware. Newspaper will not stick easily to the porous surface so the design is painted in hot wax, which can be made up by melting 3 parts of candle wax in 1 part of paraffin. This mixture must not be prepared over direct heat but always in a double container, the outer one containing hot water. Only bold designs can be executed by this method and care is necessary to prevent the splashing of wax over areas which are to remain clear.

The decorated pot is covered with an opaque coloured glaze. During the firing, the wax resist will burn away, leaving a pattern formed by areas of unglazed biscuit. These areas can be developed by the addition of painted motifs, if this is considered desirable, and followed by a further translucent glaze fire, or they can remain as contrasting areas if the biscuit is sufficiently vitrified to render it non-porous. Prepared resist liquid is also obtainable which, since it is far thinner than the wax and is applied cold, can be rather more easily controlled.

Decoration on the unfired glaze

Majolica, faience, Delft, and tin enamel are all terms used to describe ware decorated using this technique which entails painting directly onto an unfired stanniferous glaze (see Chapter 11 for opaque tin glazes). Oxides of cobalt, copper,

114

iron and manganese are all suitable pigments. The most reliable is cobalt which is why the Delft potters invariably outlined their designs in this colour. If subsidiary colours were then burnt away during firing, the resulting pattern was always complete in itself. Underglaze colours are not suitable, but some firms sell colours especially designed for majolica painting. Universal stains mixed with a little of the stanniferous glaze will serve quite well.

The pigments are ground in the usual way with water on a glass slab and applied thinly. Sufficient colour must be made ready so that the brush can be fully charged. The technique calls for deft brushwork since painting on the raw glaze is somewhat like painting on blotting paper. Indeed painting the proposed design with thinned ink on blotting paper is good practice for the beginner. If painting is carried out before the glaze has fully dried, the porosity is somewhat reduced and the job made easier.

It should be noted that any pot can be decorated by applying a prepared solution of one of the metallic colouring oxides over its unfired glaze either as brush strokes, spattering or spraying suitably masked out areas.

Glaze decoration
Interesting effects can be achieved by processes of whole or partial over-glazing. White tin glaze can be spattered, laid with a well wrung-out sponge, or poured over parts of a pot which has received a coating of coloured opaque glaze. During the firing, the two glazes will mingle and generate a white mottled pattern which is often described as a 'tin frost'. This effect can be further exploited if it is combined with the application of a resist wax. A dish, for example, could be covered with a strongly coloured glaze, a few simple brush strokes made over it with a resist liquid and the surface reglazed with a white stanniferous glaze. After firing, the resist area will stand out in pure colour against a mottled white background.

Experiments can be made by superimposing any one glaze over another; the results may be unpredictable but often interesting. Any second dipping must be applied after the first glaze has just set but has not fully dried. Precautions must also be taken to stand the pot on a spare piece of kiln shelf or a biscuited tile well covered with batt wash, in the kiln, since a double layer of glaze may well cause a glaze-run. A free-flowing glaze can be used to good effect with another of normal consistency. It is added to the top portion of a pot and encouraged to run down the side to create a 'candle-drip' effect. Glaze patterns can also be applied with a slip trailer.

Decoration on the fired glaze.

This is often described as on-glaze, overglaze or enamelling and is the type of decoration associated with everyday table ware. It entails the use of specially formulated enamel colours which consist of the same metallic oxides suitably mixed with a flux. They are fired onto the glaze at a temperature between 740°C and 850°C depending on the type of ware. During this fixing, the glaze becomes slightly softened. The permitted firing temperature for the enamel can therefore be higher if it has been applied to a stoneware or porcelain glaze. The relatively low temperature of the enamelling kiln allows a very wide palette of colours to be used. Additional metal oxides, which would break up at normal kiln temperatures, can be used – reds, pink and the more delicate pastel shades are all possible. Unlike the underglaze colours, they are not fully sealed by the glaze and are liable, after years of use, to wear away.

Patterns in enamel can be applied in numerous ways, many being outside the province of the home potter. Any review of pottery decoration would, however, be incomplete without some information being given of the more basic techniques.

Direct brush painting
The on-glaze colours are ground on a glass with a little pure turpentine – white spirit will not do – to which is added a few drops of fat oil. Camel hair brushes used for painting must be cleaned between each colour in a small jar of turpentine. The

medium permits considerable control over the brush strokes and a gradation of line and colour. China painting, as it is often called, is a complete study in itself and any student interested in this style of decoration should consult specialist books devoted to the art.

Ground laying
The glazed surface is thoroughly cleaned with a little whiting powder, and is then coated with a thin layer of a special ground laying oil which has been thinned down with pure turpentine. It is best applied with a soft wide flat brush and if on a plate or similar object, spun on with the aid of a banding wheel. An even layer is essential and ridges of the oil must be avoided. When this layer has become tacky, it is lightly dabbed all over with a silk boss, made by covering a wad of cottonwool with a piece of silk as for applying French polish. This evens the layer of oil. If working properly, the boss should emit a little clicking sound as it leaves the oil. Enamel colour is then dusted on, using a small powder puff. This will adhere to the sticky surface. After this has hardened, a pattern can be drawn in through the colour in what we have already met as the sgraffito method. If applied to a white surface the scratched lines, too, will appear white. Tremendous detail is possible if a variety of scratching tools is used, indeed the detail can be every bit as fine as that obtainable on a scraper board. A check should be made on completion of the design to ensure that enamel colours are not adhering to areas which are to be left clear.

Lustres
Metallic bands can be spun onto glazed ware in the form of liquid lustres, but these are very expensive. One lustre technique will help to illustrate the universality of the resist principle. A pattern can be painted onto a plate using thick vermillion water colour paint as a resist agent. When this is dry the whole surface can be covered with a silver or other liquid lustre. The enamel fire which follows will burn away the paint and the pattern, after cleaning with a little powdered whiting, stands out in the basic plate colour.

Screen printing

Many of the patterns in commercial tableware are applied as transfers. Amateur interest has been growing in recent years in the making of slide-off transfers from original designs by silk-screen printing. The making and use of a silk screen is covered in the *Beginners Guide to Fabric Dying and Printing* published in this series.

Underglaze or on-glaze enamels are ground with screen printing medium and applied through the screen to 'Thermaflat' transfer paper. When fully dry, the design is overprinted with 'Covercoat' through a 60's mesh screen. This application should overlap the printed area by about $\frac{1}{32}$ inch (1 mm). This layer, too, must be left aside to become fully air-dried. The paper bearing the pattern is soaked for a minute or so in water, after which the 'Covercoat' with the pattern will slide free from the paper backing and can be moulded in position to the shape of the pot. Pressure must be carefully applied through a dry cloth or blotting paper to render tight adhesion to the ware and to ensure that there are no air bubbles between transfer and pot. On irregular surfaces the use of a steamed towel can prove helpful in ensuring perfect adhesion. Multicoloured designs can be made by multiplying the number of screens, but each colour must be perfectly dry before the next is laid.

10

Tiles

Tile-making can be a very rewarding activity, especially if the potter is sufficiently versatile to combine it with other crafts such as woodworking. Delightful combination pieces can be produced. For example a tile could be inlaid in a hardwood cheese board matching a design on a ceramic butter dish. A coffee table could be designed to be fitted with a tiled surface and, if tiles in two contrasting colours and about 2 inches (50 mm) square were laid as a chequer board, the table could be used for the playing of chess perhaps with ceramic chessmen. More ambitious projects could include the making of 'spot' tiles for a fireplace surround. Although traditionally of square shape, it is now quite usual to see tiles made in other regular shapes, such as the hexagon, which link easily to cover a complete surface area.

The great problem in all tile making is that of warping. As tiles dry, they tend to buckle since the edges dry more quickly than at the centre and consequently will not bed down flat when used. Industrial tiles are heavily machine-pressed in a metal mould and made from clay which is barely damp and so need little more drying after making. It will be obvious that the larger the tile the greater will be the effect of buckling, so from the amateur potter's point of view, it is advisable to make relatively small tiles no larger than 4 square inches (100 mm). To finish with a tile of this size, it will need to be made larger to allow for subsequent shrinkage on drying and firing. The amount will vary slightly from one body to another, but as a rule of thumb it is usual to allow

⅛ inch (3 mm) for every inch (25 mm) of size so that the 4 inch (100 mm) tile will need to have an initial measurement of 4½ × 4½ inches (112 × 112 mm). In general, a good thickness is ⅜ inch (10 mm) to ½ inch (12 mm).

Keeping the body open will do much to minimise warping. A fireclay body is very suitable, but as much grog as possible should be worked into whatever clay is used. Having the same object in mind, great importance must be attached to the manner in which the tiles are dried after making, the aim being to allow the whole tile to dry at the same rate. Turning is important and the tiles should be stacked in staggered rows, resting one edge upon the next so that air will be able to circulate freely on either side. Moreover, the combined weight of the pile will tend to hold the edges down.

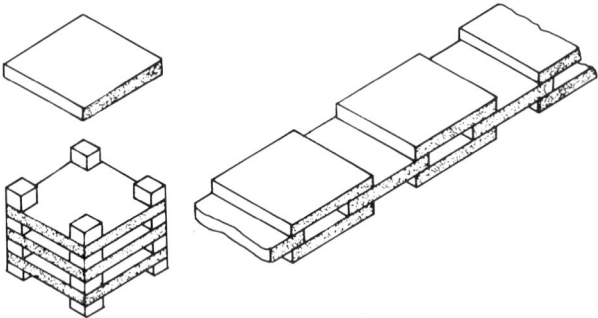

Figure 10.1. Methods of stacking green tiles to dry

Alternatively, they may be built up in vertical piles and separated by small even spacers at the corners, in similar fashion to the sticks used in wood seasoning (Figure 10.1).

Another possibility is to dry the tiles on a stout, rigid, wire grid. Badly supported wire netting should be avoided.

Methods of making tiles

Individual tiles can be *cut with a palette knife* or other thin blade from a slab of prepared clay, rolled out between slats to the correct thickness. A template cut in card or, even better, in hardboard should be used as a guide. *Metal tile cutters* are obtainable in a number of shapes and sizes from pottery suppliers. These work on a spring-operated ejection principle and closely resemble the wafer-making appliance used by an ice-cream vendor (Figure 10.2).

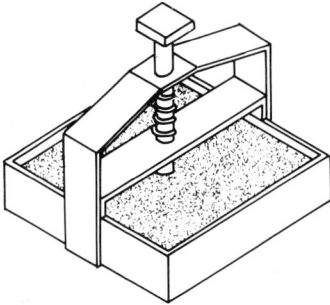

Figure 10.2. Metal tile cutter

The shapes are cut from the usual rolled-out slab of clay.

Single tiles can be made within a *wooden tray mould* consisting of four pieces of wood joined to act as limiting walls for the clay. They should be planed to the required thickness of the tile and either tacked together or dry-jointed to facilitate removal (Figure 10.3). The frame is placed on a flat surface which has been covered with a sheet of paper to prevent sticking and the clay is pressed into it, a little at a

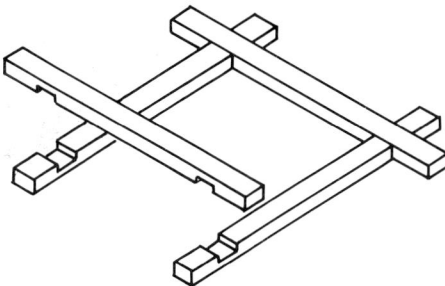

Figure 10.3. Single wooden tile mould

121

time, to avoid trapping pockets of air. It should be slightly over-filled and the top levelled with the aid of a wooden slat, ruler or similar straight edge, working from side to side and diagonally from each corner in turn. Both the straight edge and the tile should be kept damp. When the tile has hardened enough to handle, the frame can be removed together with any paper still adhering to the back, and the tile left to dry.

The best way of making a number of tiles is to combine the first two methods described and to make a larger frame of sufficient size to enclose ten or a dozen identical tiles. The frame should be lightly screwed to a base of water-resistant

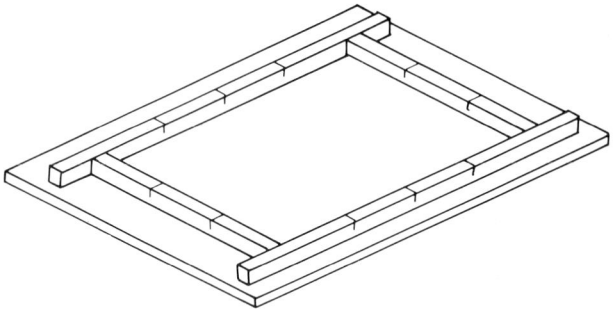

Figure 10.4. Multiple wooden tile mould

composition-board and its sides marked with a saw to indicate the limits of each tile. The inside of this box mould must be lined with paper or dusted with fine sand or grog to prevent sticking. The whole tray is filled with the grogged clay and levelled. It is then an easy matter to lay a straight edge across the frame in both directions at the marked positions and to make knife cuts against it (Figure 10.4).

Plaster moulds are very useful for making a number of tiles which are to be decorated with a raised or incised pattern. Consideration of this technique raises the whole question of tile decoration.

Decorating tiles

The many decorative techniques already described can all be employed in the decoration of tiles, but because of their flat nature and of the fact that the glazed surface will remain flat during firing, some techniques can be further developed. Patterns can either be designed to stand complete or can require a group of tiles for completion.

Encaustic tiles
These were much used in the Middle Ages for the floors of cathedrals and abbeys and incorporated an inlay technique which rendered the pattern safe from obliteration by the constant tread of feet. Areas of the tile are cut out to form the pattern and, after being coated with slip, are filled with a contrasting clay which must possess a similar coefficient of expansion and be similarly grogged. Careful filling is necessary to avoid the formation of air locks. The whole tile must be levelled with a damp straight edge. At this stage, the surface will appear smudged and the pattern will only come to life when the clay has dried and the surface has been lightly scraped with a sharp edge, using no water. A final rub with very fine glasspaper when the tile is fully dried is also useful. Cutting out a number of matching tiles of this type can be somewhat tedious and an easier method is to make a plaster mould.

Making a plaster tile mould
Any ordinary clay is rolled out to create a half inch (12 mm) thick slab of clay from which an accurate tile is cut. Another is made about $3/16$ inch (5 mm) thick. When both are leather-hard, the proposed motif, which has already been accurately drawn on a piece of paper, is traced onto both the tile and the thinner clay. The design is then cut carefully out of the thinner clay with a small knife. It may be made up of one organic unit or of a number of separate entities. This cut-out pattern is then stuck on the tile with a little slip in the position already marked. The sides of the raised pattern must be trimmed and modelled to a slight upward taper to allow for

'draw'. Final smoothing can be helped by a small damp sponge or soft paint brush.

The tile is now placed on a flat surface and a wooden frame, or a small casting box may be made to enclose it. The width of the frame should be sufficient to include the thickness of the tile plus about 1 inch (25 mm). All the joints in the box are then sealed with clay and plaster of Paris mixed and poured to cover the tile by about ¾ inch (19 mm). This will form the waste-mould, the pattern appearing on it in a hollow form. It must now be thoroughly soap-sized, reset in the box, and a plaster reverse made. When this has set, the two plasters can be separated in the usual way by plunging them into a bowl of water and pulling them apart. The half required is that bearing the original motif in raised form.

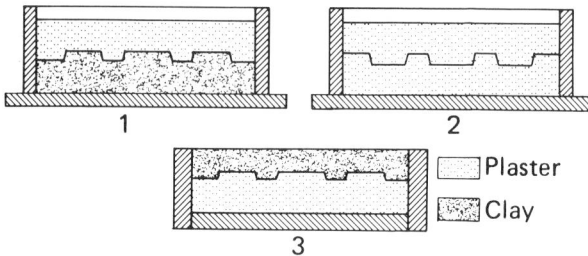

Figure 10.5. Stages in making a plaster mould for encaustic tiles

A more accurate moulding box must now be constructed by screwing the sides to a base which exactly fits around the plaster. These screws can be loosened when the time comes to remove the completed tile from the box. In order that each subsequent tile is of the same thickness, the sides must be prepared to a width which will be the sum of the thickness of the wooden base, plus that of the plaster mould and of the finished tile (Figure 10.5).

When the box has been prepared, the plaster cast is placed in the bottom, the remainder of the box carefully press-filled with grogged clay, and the top levelled. When the tile is removed it will bear the necessary recesses which can then be filled, as before, with the contrasting clay. It should be noted that if the waste cast is substituted and the tile pressed, it will emerge bearing the motif in relief. Used in this manner the moulding box serves the same purpose as the wooden die which was used by the early monks.

An extension of the slip-trailing technique
If specific areas of a pattern are outlined with a slip-trailed wall, they can, after the tile has been biscuited, be filled with a variety of coloured, transparent or opaque glazes. The trailed lines will keep the various glazes apart. Alternatively, the 'wells' can be filled with broken glass or cullet. The resultant effect is reminiscent of cloisonné enamel, the trailed line taking the place of the wire.

Silk-screen printing
Silk-screen printing is very suitable for the repetitive decoration of a number of matching tiles. As they are flat there is no need for an intermediate transfer.

Colours or a resist medium can be applied directly onto the biscuited tiles through the screen. Underglaze colours are thoroughly ground with a screen printing medium which can be either oil- or water-based. The tiles must be thoroughly dry, clean, and free from dust and grease. If the oil-based medium is used, a preliminary burning-off fire will be required before glazing.

Small tiles known as tesserae can be cut from rolled-out clay slabs, fired in odd spaces of the kiln and used to create simple mosaics.

11

Glazes and glazing

Glazing is an integral part of pottery-making and is very satisfying. Before dealing with the process in detail it is important to examine the reasons why it is carried out. Since the clay has not been fired to the point of vitrification, earthenware is porous. Glazing an earthenware pot, at least on one side, is therefore a practical necessity to render it waterproof, but it can at the same time serve to make it much more attractive. This is the essence of good design, a true merging of the functional and the aesthetic.

Stoneware or porcelain, if fired to its maturing temperature, becomes non-porous and therefore requires no glaze to make it watertight. Why then is it customary for such pots to be glazed? In the first instance, to make them more attractive. Glazing can impart life, colour and a variety of interesting surface textures and complement the form. A good glaze can never hide a badly shaped pot but can do much to add quality to a well-designed one. But here, too, there are practical and technical reasons. An unglazed pot, especially if used as tableware, is difficult to keep clean and its surface tends to collect dirt and stains. Glaze is therefore applied for reasons of hygiene. Adding a transparent glaze is also an excellent way in which to seal in any decoration which has been applied to the biscuit. One of the great advantages of the underglaze work is that it is completely covered by a layer of glass and cannot therefore show signs of wear however much the article is used and cleaned.

The constituents of a glaze

The basic ingredient of a glaze is silica (Silicon dioxide) which occurs in the form of flint or quartz. It can also be found as glassy crystals in the sand of most beaches, and in the combined state in minerals such as feldspar, Cornish stone and other silicates.

Silica melts at an extremely high temperature (1600–1750°C) to form a viscous liquid or glass. Temperatures in this region are well above the working limit of the potter's kiln. In order to bring the melting point down to within kilning range, the silica is combined with certain other substances which are known as fluxes, because they cause the silica to flow. It is not imperative for the craftsman to fully understand the scientific explanation of the manner in which the fluxes function, but for those with a scientific bent this is outlined in the appendix on page 166.

Suffice it to say that the flux dissolves the silica, and the glass so formed is a solution which freezes as a glaze at normal temperatures.

Adding the flux solves the temperature question but another problem still exists, for a glaze made up of a mixture of silica and flux, when molten, would fail to adhere to the pot surface. To build a successful glaze, then, a third ingredient must be added to increase the viscosity of the molten silica and so prevent it from running into a pool at the base of the pot. This is alumina (Aluminium oxide), which is one of the main constituents of clay, and explains why glaze recipes include either China clay or ball clay.

Variety in ceramic glazes is brought about by variation in the materials chosen as fluxes and by varying the proportions of silica, flux and alumina.

Classification of glazes

Several criteria are commonly used to categorise glazes. One is to label them according to the temperature at which they mature, as in the table below:

Glaze type	Maturing temperature range
Soft earthenware	900–960°C
Normal earthenware	1050–1100°C
Medium stoneware	1200–1220°C
High-fired stoneware	1230–1300°C

An alternative means of classification is to group glazes according to the type of flux used, and in a more general way, grouping can be based on physical appearance – a glaze may be described as transparent, opaque or matt. Finally, all glazes can belong to one of two categories namely raw, or fritted. It should be noted that these terms may be used together to give a fuller description, for example, 'an opaque, leadless, earthenware glaze'.

Fluxing agents

These are all metallic oxides. *Lead oxide* (Red Lead) has been used as a flux for many centuries and is capable of reducing the melting point of the silica to its lower limits. Consequently, it is the natural choice as a flux for soft earthenware (Majolica) glazes. Few fluxes are wholly satisfactory when used in isolation and lead is one of these. Medieval potters followed the practice of dusting their pots, whilst still damp, with lead sulphide (Galena) which reacted with the silica and alumina in the clay body to form a grey-green glaze. Lead also benefits the glaze in other ways: brilliance and sparkle are attained due to the high index of refraction and a low surface tension allows a lead glaze to heal over blisters and any drying cracks. Any tendency towards surface crystallisation of the glass is minimised and the colour response is excellent. There is, however, one important snag. Lead can be released from the glaze if it remains in contact with an acid. These conditions can be realised if lead-glazed tableware is used to contain acidic foods or drinks. How this health hazard can be minimised is fully discussed under the heading of *Fritting* (page 130).

128

If earthenware can be fired to its traditional range (1050–1100°C), other fluxes such as the oxides of potassium, sodium and calcium can share the role with lead. Two or more are usually built into the glaze to make for a good fit (see page 138). The benefits to be derived from lead also operate in such mixed flux glazes. The alkalis, soda and potash, can be used as fluxes in earthenware glazes without the addition of lead. Such glazes give a good colour response which can be very different from that obtained by using the same colouring agent in a lead glaze, for example the beautiful turquoise blue produced when copper oxide is added to an alkaline glaze. The difficulties which arise in designing and using alkaline glazes are dealt with under the topic of fritting.

Lead becomes volatile at temperatures between 1150°C and 1200°C and leaves the glass, so it can never be used in stoneware glazes. These rely on the oxides of sodium, potassium, magnesium, calcium and lithium. So-called Bristol glazes incorporate zinc oxide as a flux.

Sources of the fluxing agents

Many are present in naturally occurring minerals as Table 11.1 shows.

Table 11.1

Mineral	Flux present	Composition Alumina	Silica
Potash feldspar	1 part potassium oxide	1 part	6 parts
Soda feldspar	1 part sodium oxide	1 part	6 parts
Nepheline syenite	1 part potassium oxide 3 parts sodium oxide	4 parts	8 parts
*Cornish stone	1 part potassium oxide	1 part	8 parts
Petalite	1 part lithium oxide	1 part	8 parts
Spodumene	1 part lithium oxide	1 part	4 parts
Steatite (talc)	3 parts magnesium oxide	—	4 parts

*Some suppliers offer mineralised stone as an alternative.
Dolomite contains 1 part calcium carbonate + 1 part magnesium carbonate.

An examination of these compositions will show that, apart from dolomite and talc, they all contain both alumina and silica as well as the flux and so provide the three requisites of a glaze.

The glaze builder must take note of all the compounds of which the mineral is made up and, when using it to provide a specific quantity of the required flux, remember that large quantities of both alumina and silica are being simultaneously added (see Appendix 1, page 166). All these mineral sources are insoluble in water. In many cases the flux can be added in the form of a chemical powder. The following are insoluble in water:

Lead oxide (red lead)

Lead carbonate (white lead)

Calcium carbonate (whiting)

Barium carbonate (witherite)

Lithium carbonate

Magnesium carbonate

Zinc oxide

The following are soluble in water:

Potassium carbonate (Pearl ash)

Sodium carbonate (Soda ash)

Borax

It may seem odd to beginners with little experience of chemistry to discover that fluxes are often supplied in the form of the carbonate of the metal and not, as has been previously stated, in the form of the oxide. This is explained by the fact that, when heated in the kiln, carbonates loose carbon dioxide gas, which is dissipated through the kiln vent, and the carbonates are converted to the appropriate oxides. For example:

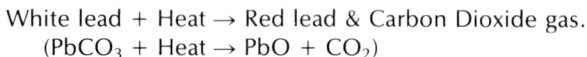

White lead + Heat → Red lead & Carbon Dioxide gas.
$(PbCO_3 + Heat \rightarrow PbO + CO_2)$

Fritting

Glaze is prepared for use by suspending the powdered ingredients in water. When the porous biscuit is dipped into the suspension it absorbs the water and an even layer of the glaze itself is deposited onto the surface. This works well for most glaze substances, which as we have seen, are predominantly insoluble in water.

The alkaline fluxes, soda and potash, are safe if introduced as feldspar or syenite but if extra soda or potash is desirable it is impractical to add more of these minerals as this would, at the same time, bring in an excess of both alumina and silica. The best way round this is to introduce the extra soda and potash in the form of pure compounds such as borax, sodium carbonate or potassium carbonate. All these are unfortunately soluble in water, and if used, are carried by the water into the porous clay pot. The result is that the deposited glaze, deprived of its flux, refuses to melt and the pot itself, which is made up of alumina and silica, will tend to flux.

To overcome this problem, the soluble compounds are melted together with a portion of the insoluble ingredients in the recipe. The molten mixture is then run off into cold water where it solidifies into glass beads which are then reground. The resultant powder is known as a frit. In this form the soluble materials are rendered insoluble and can be reintroduced with the balance of insoluble substances specified in the recipe to be used as a normal glaze. Frits are available from potter's suppliers and their composition is usually quoted.

Fritting can also help to solve the problem of lead solubility, to which reference has already been made. If raw lead oxide is fritted with the silica and some alumina in the recipe, the lead is rendered far less soluble in acid and the glaze becomes safe to use on food containers. This explains the meaning of the term 'Low-solubility (LS) glaze'.

As well as being the answer to two serious glaze problems, fritting is of value in another way. Fritted glazes are often more fusible and scratch-resistant. They are also less apt to bubble and crawl since impurities and gases such as carbon dioxide have already been released in the making of the frit.

Opacity

Glazes can be made opaque by adding up to 10 per cent of tin oxide to the recipe. Such glazes are pure white and were the stock-in-trade of the Delft Majolica potters. Zirconium oxide or zirconium silicate (zircon) can be used to a maximum of 10–15 per cent of the total glaze, as an alternative to make the glaze opaque but the result is a creamy, rather than milky, colour. Tin oxide is a very expensive material and it is now common to replace at least a part of the quantity added by zirconium oxide. Some glazes, notably those incorporating dolomite, are inherently opaque, as are many of the celadons. The use of 10 per cent of titanium, or of its impure form, rutile, results in a creamy white opaque glaze with a semi-matt surface.

Matting a glaze

Suppliers list matting agents which can be added to a glaze at the rate of 15–20 per cent, depending on the degree of mattness required. However, the final result of these tends to appear rather scummy. Alternatively, the addition of 20 per cent of whiting will produce a similar effect. Matting is, however, best achieved by manipulating the flux/alumina/silica/ratio. The silica should be kept low, the alumina as high as possible and 25 – 30 per cent of the fluxes should comprise zinc oxide. A glaze embodying these principles is listed in Appendix 2 (page 174).

Boric oxide

Boric oxide is unique in playing a dual role when introduced into a glaze. In some ways it behaves in a similar manner to alumina, but, like silica, it also combines with the fluxes to form a glass. Boric oxide is normally added in the form of borax, which is made up of 1 part sodium oxide, 2 parts boric oxide and 10 parts water. The combination of these two oxides serves to soften a glaze and lower its melting point to a similar extent as lead oxide. Leadless earthenware glazes are thus all boron-based (Labelled 'L' in suppliers' lists).

If both lead and boric oxide are added, a glaze can have an extremely low point of fusion, but is not of good quality. Since borax is soluble, it must be introduced as a frit. Boracic glazes give a good colour response similar, in the case of copper oxide, to alkaline glazes. Calcium borate is one source of boric oxide which is insoluble and so can be used in a raw boro-silicate glaze. Commonly known as colemanite, it contains 2 parts lime, 3 parts boric oxide and 5 parts water, the latter evaporating as steam in the firing. Colemanite is also available in frit form (see page 130).

Colouring a glaze

Colouring agents are all oxides of metals, but, as with fluxes, they can also be added to the glaze as carbonates. The oxides possess stronger colouring action and are consequently used in smaller proportions. Various factors contribute to the colour of the final product.

First, stained transparent glaze will allow the natural colour of the clay pot to show through and a white biscuit will obviously reflect more of the glaze colour than a red one. If an opaque glaze is used the colour of the underlying biscuit will cease to exert such a dominating influence. Resultant colour is also affected by the fluxes used in the glaze.

Yet another important factor is the atmosphere prevalent in the kiln. Heat is generated in all types of fuel-burning kilns by the combustion of the gas, wood, coal or oil, a process for which oxygen, derived from the air, is essential. By-products, such as carbon dioxide and carbon monoxide, escape through the flue. Provided the air vents remain open, sufficient oxygen will be available for complete burning and the kiln atmosphere is said to be a clean or oxidising one. If, however, the air intake is restricted, combustion ceases to be complete and smoke forms inside the kiln. This has an important effect on the colouring pigments of the glaze, for if the burning process is hungry for oxygen, it will seek out sources other than the air, such as the metallic oxides. The oxides of copper and iron, because of their particular chemical properties, have traditionally provided the potter with the lovely celadon and scarlet 'sang de boeuf' glazes.

The introduction of a little chemistry is necessary in order to understand how changes in colour can be brought about by a smoky kiln atmosphere. There are two oxides of copper, cupric (copper II) and cuprous (copper I). Cupric oxide remains stable in an oxidising atmosphere and gives the typical green colour response. If, however, the atmosphere is deficient in oxygen, some of that from the cupric oxide is used for combustion which is thus reduced to the cuprous form and produces a blood-red colour.

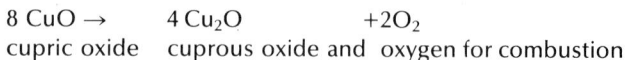

$$8\,CuO \rightarrow \qquad 4\,Cu_2O \qquad\qquad +2O_2$$
cupric oxide   cuprous oxide and oxygen for combustion

A similar reaction takes place in the case of iron, which is normally used in the red, ferric oxide (iron III) form, resulting in a honey-brown tone. In a reducing atmosphere the ferric oxide looses some of its oxygen and is reduced to the ferrous (iron II) state, giving rise to the unique celadon greens.

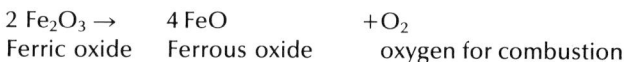

$$2\,Fe_2O_3 \rightarrow \qquad 4\,FeO \qquad\qquad +O_2$$
Ferric oxide   Ferrous oxide   oxygen for combustion

It will be obvious that for these changes to occur the pots must be open to the changing type of atmosphere. It is not easy to create a reducing atmosphere in a muffle kiln. The clean atmosphere of an electric kiln cannot really be used for reduction. Attempts have been made to overcome this limitation by introducing combustible material into the kiln, but they are far from practical and the elements are liable to damage. A reducing atmosphere will ruin a glaze containing lead.

Using colouring oxides

It must be emphasised that colours vary with the contents of the glaze recipe, with firing and, since some colouring agents volatilise in the kiln, with the range of other glazes in the batch. For example, chrome oxide volatilises at temperatures above 1000°C and, if added to a glaze on one of the pots in a

134

kiln, can turn others containing tin oxide, pink. Table 11.2 gives some indication of the colour range which can be expected from the more predictable oxides, but others, notably the oxides of chrome and nickel, produce such variable effects depending upon the presence of other ingredients that they are difficult to tabulate, and experience will prove the best tutor. It is interesting to experiment with mixtures of the colouring pigments, testing small amounts on scrap pieces of biscuit in odd corners of the kiln. Raw colours such as copper-green or cobalt blue can, for instance, be modified to produce a whole range of intermediate tones. Iron chromate is useful as a greying agent if more subdued colours are preferred. Glaze stains are available from suppliers but it will prove far more exciting to work from basic raw materials. Smaller percentages of the colouring oxides should be added to a matt glaze.

Wood-ash glazes

Ash, resulting from the complete combustion of wood contains inorganic compounds, notably silica and metallic oxides. Wood ash therefore contains fluxes, some of which are alkaline and fugitive, and silica, but few contain alumina in any quantity. Used alone, therefore, ash rarely makes a satisfactory glaze and must be incorporated into a recipe with feldspar, china clay, china stone, or ball clay. Ash from different plant species varies considerably in composition so experimentation is in every case necessary to determine its fluxing and refractory potential in order to frame a satisfactory recipe. Forty per cent ash, 40 per cent feldspar and 20 per cent ball clay forms a good basis for testing.

If the student wishes to prepare some home-produced ash to use in a glaze, it must first be dry sieved to remove any large pieces of unburnt material, then soaked in water and the mixture passed through a coarse lawn to remove the smaller residue. After settling, the liquid must be poured off. Care is necessary as the liquid contains soluble alkalis and will be caustic. The remaining ash slurry is again mixed with

Table 11.2

	Lead glazes	Soft leadless glazes	High temperature glazes Oxidising	Reducing	Remarks
Red oxide of iron (Fe_2O_3)	1–6%: pale amber to reddish brown	1–5%: Browns	1–7%: light to dark browns	2%: celadons. 10%: very dark brown to black	Never use with Zinc oxide. Can be introduced as impure form which will often produce speckles.
Copper oxide (CuO) or copper carbonate ($CuCO_3$)	1–4%: grass greens. Metallic above 5%	2% gives turquoise blue in alkaline glaze & blue green in boracic glazes	1–4%: green	0.5%: scarlet	Acts as flux if used in higher percentages. Makes lead more soluble and is not advised for tableware. Pink in dolomite glazes.

Oxide				
Black cobalt oxide (Co_3O_4) or cobalt carbonate ($CoCO_3$)	0.5–2%: blue	0.5–3%: brilliant blue	0.1–1%: blue	0.1–1%: blue	Extremely powerful agent. The oxide must be well ground to avoid speckle. Can become green in glaze containing rutile. Pink/mauve in dolomite glaze.
Manganese dioxide (MnO_2) or manganese carbonate ($MnCO_3$)	5–10%: purple brown	1–8%: mauve, plum	1–8%: volatile at high temperatures, sometimes giving a grey	1–8%: grey-green	Apt to blister. Very strong fluxing power. With iron can produce lustre. Pink/mauve in dolomite glaze.

clean water, stirred well and allowed to settle a second time before pouring away the surplus water. Further washings can be made, but at each wash more fluxes will be removed and the ash will become more refractory. The final wet ash must be thoroughly dried before being stored in a glass jar.

Wood-ash glazes require firing to stoneware temperatures to develop the subtle colours, and for the finest effects, the kiln atmosphere must be a reducing one.

Glaze fit

Both clay and glaze are subject, like metals, to expansion or contraction with varying kiln temperatures. Ideally, the coefficient of expansion of the clay body should be very slightly higher than the glaze so that the latter is always compressed. If, on cooling, the layer of glaze shrinks considerably more than the clay, it will be subject, like drying mud, to crazing producing a network of fine cracks in the glaze. If this occurs on porous biscuit, such as earthenware, the pot will not be watertight. Alternatively, if the glaze shrinks too little compared with the clay, it will tend to peel off, especially along edges. The former condition can usually be corrected by increasing the silica content of the body and firing the biscuit to a higher temperature. Conversely, peeling can be reduced by lowering the silica content of the body and the firing temperature of the biscuit.

Choosing first glazes

Beginners attending a busy evening class may well have to choose their glazes from a ready-mixed stock selection. For those with home facilities, standard transparent and opaque glazes are available from suppliers. The beginner may well be advised to take advantage of these, especially as a catalogue usually indicates bodies and glazes which fit, but the desire to experiment, firstly by adding colouring oxides to the basic glazes, and then by weighing out and preparing glazes from recipes gleaned from books or practical potters, will inevitably follow. Tremendous excitement and motivation will be generated from opening the glaze kiln and examining the results obtained. A record should be kept giving details of all trials together with a final assessment of their quality. Building and manipulating a glaze requires rather more scientific understanding and much testing.

Preparation of glazes

Stock glaze powders
These are sold with a small degree of moisture to prevent inhalation of the powder and are therefore often lumpy. The powder should be sprinkled into water and allowed to stand to help disperse the lumps. At this stage, more water than will finally be necessary can be used. Stir the mixture to give an even suspension of the powder in the water. Next pass the mixture through a 120 mesh phosphor bronze sieve using a lawn brush. The excess water will have produced a slop glaze which is far too runny, but wear and tear on the lawn will have been minimised.

Now allow the mixture to settle for an hour or so. The insoluble ingredients of the glaze will sink to the bottom and the excess water can be ladled or syphoned off. Judging the amount of water in the final glaze slip has ultimately to be a matter of personal experience. Consistency will depend upon the porosity of the biscuit ware: the greater the porosity the less water required. Generally speaking, stoneware glazes need to be applied more thickly than those used on earthenware. Moreover, the thickness of the glaze can often result in considerable changes in both colour and texture. Trials will indicate the optimum thickness to use. On average, the consistency will be similar to that of thin cream. More specifically, a pint of slop glaze should weigh around 30 oz.

It is wise to test the viscosity of the glaze, before use on a full batch of pots. This can be done by dipping a piece of broken clay biscuit into the stirred glaze and allowing it to dry. If this takes a long while and leaves a series of water runs, water should be removed. If it dries immediately, leaving a very thick layer of glaze, the glaze must be diluted. A glaze of the correct consistency should, when scratched, leave a definite, clean line without flaking on either side.

Making a glaze from a recipe
Recipes are usually given as percentage amounts and quantities quoted can be interpreted as either ounces or grams. They can, of course, be multiplied to make up any quantity of glaze.

Weigh out the ingredients carefully and then, as before, disperse them in water and sieve. A pestle and mortar helps to grind the dry ingredients together prior to adding to the water, especially if colouring agents, such as cobalt oxide, are included. It is a good idea to tick off the ingredients on the recipe list as they are added to avoid omissions or duplications. Plastic bowls are ideal for glaze preparation.

Some glazes will be found to settle very quickly and form a very hard layer at the bottom of the bucket. This condition can be alleviated by adding 1 per cent of bentonite to the glaze recipe and, after suspension in the water, a saturated solution of calcium chloride at the rate of 3–4 drops per full bucket or pro rata according to the amount of glaze being mixed. This saturated solution can be prepared by dissolving the maximum possible amount of the chemical in a few fluid ounces of hot water, allowing it to stand, and then pouring off the liquid (which is the saturated solution) above the residue.

Test-pieces

Testing a glaze on a flat tile gives a poor indication of how it will behave on the vertical side of a pot. It is good practice, therefore, to make up and fire pieces of biscuit as shown in the diagram (Figure 11.1). Should the glaze run, it will not spill onto the kiln shelf, and plenty of space is available for

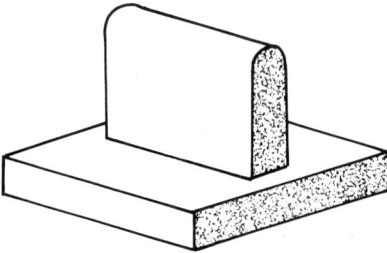

Figure 11.1. Glaze test piece made up from slabs of clay and biscuited

details of the glaze which can be written on the base using a brush charged with a little cobalt oxide ground on a glass with water.

Glazing procedure

The method adopted to glaze a pot will depend on its size, shape and complexity, and to a very large extent on the amount of glaze available. An amateur who has just a few pots to cover in any one type of glaze will need to adopt a different approach to that of a potter, producing a large batch of one particular item. It is always necessary to weigh up the factors involved and to decide beforehand the best method to adopt for glazing each individual pot.

In all methods, the aim must be to coat the pot with an even layer of glaze. The correct thickness is not easy to prescribe and ultimately is a decision which can only be made by experience. The amount of water to be added to a glaze will depend, in large measure, upon the porosity of the biscuit. In a mixed kiln, this may vary considerably between one pot and another, but if one specific body is being regularly used, it will pay always to biscuit it at the same temperature so that optimum glaze cover, once established, can be maintained. Even so, factors such as the thickness of a clay wall, may result in variation in glaze absorption. Glaze will probably need to be made thicker when the biscuit is a

141

hard-baked earthenware than when a stoneware glaze is being applied to a relatively soft-baked pot. Generally speaking, transparent glazes need somewhat thinner application than do opaque ones.

A few odd pieces of clay baked in the biscuit kiln, can serve as test pieces, being dipped into the glaze to make a quick check on the thickness of the deposited layer. They will also provide a good indication of the speed of drying. If it remains wet for too long, the resultant runs will leave bare channels on the pot which are difficult to remedy.

Speed is a key factor since this, in the last instance, controls the thickness of the glaze layer. The necessary co-ordination of hand movements is not easy and the beginner is advised to practise the various methods described using previously glazed ware and water until the knack has been mastered. This will build up confidence.

Dipping

If a reasonable quantity of glaze is available, articles such as shallow bowls, saucers and dishes can simply be passed through the liquid. Hold the pot by as few fingers as possible, gripping either the two sides of the rim or the rim and the foot and pass it into the glaze, one edge of the rim serving as a leading edge. When the pot is completely immersed it is quickly brought out again on the opposite side. The pot should pass through the liquid in a curved sweep. Once free of the glaze, the pot should be tilted on its side and turned, first one way, and then the other, to allow excess slop to drain away, and then placed on a wire grid or an old stilt to dry. Any fingermarks must be touched up immediately, either using a soft brush or a finger well charged with glaze.

Swilling and pouring

Deeper pots such as vases, should have the inside glazed first by a swilling process. Pour a quantity of the glaze into the pot, then, holding it between the two hands tilt it gently and rotate slowly so that the glaze which is running out, comes into contact with the whole of the inside surface. (Figure 11.2). When this has been achieved, the pot should be turned, first one way, and then the other, until drainage is complete to prevent run-back and the formation of thick blobs of glaze on the rim. When sufficiently dry, any glaze which has spilled onto the outside should be removed.

The outer surface can now be coated in one of two ways. If there is sufficient depth of glaze in the container, the pot can be held at the foot with two fingers and thumb and pushed, mouth downwards, into the glaze. This is where curved turning (see page 50), can be of so much help. An air-lock will be created, as in a diving bell, and the inside will receive no

Figure 11.2. Swilling the inside of a biscuited pot with glaze

further glaze. It must be lifted out slowly, especially as it breaks the surface, and dried in an upright position.

If only a small quantity of glaze is available, the outside is best glazed by pouring. The pot is held at the foot by two fingers and thumb of the left hand so that it hangs, mouth downwards, tilted over a bowl. Rotate the pot slowly in the left hand and pour a steady stream of glaze over it from a full jug held in the right hand until completely coated. A few extra turns in both directions, for purposes of drainage, will ensure a smoothly glazed rim before the pot is stood in an upright position to dry (Figure 11.3).

Inverting the pot can be made easier by supporting the now dry inside with the fingers of the right hand. Any finger-marks must be re-touched immediately. In many ways, this is the most suitable procedure for the amateur but it needs practice to co-ordinate the turning activity of one hand and the pouring process of the other. The secret lies in maintaining an even pour over one position; the temptation to turn both hands will spell disaster.

If a pot is too large and heavy to be held in one hand, the pot can be inverted on two wooden slats placed across the

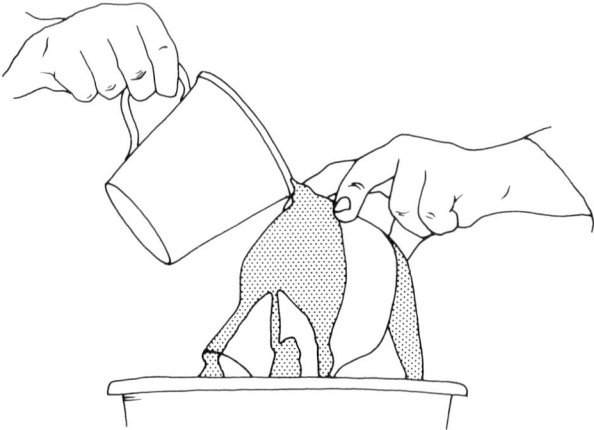

Figure 11.3. Glazing the outside of a pot by pouring

mouth of a bowl. The bowl itself is then centred on a banding wheel so that the whole assembly can be turned with the left hand as the glaze is poured. It is essential that the jug be fairly large and well-filled with glaze as it cannot be replenished half-way through the operation.

Spraying
The use of a spray gun to distribute a glaze layer must only be considered when a ventilated booth is available. Sprayed glaze, freely discharged into the atmosphere of a pottery, can create a serious health hazard. If the pot is placed on a

banding wheel within the booth, an even coating on all surfaces can more easily be effected. Spraying on glaze can have its advantages, especially when used over underglazed paint or crayon where it minimises the danger of smudging, but it can also present problems. Too heavy a burst in one specific area can cause glaze runs and it is not always easy to estimate the thickness of the applied layer.

Painting
Where only very small quantities of glaze are available or when the object to be glazed is very small, glaze can be painted on with a large soft brush. It is not easy to produce an evenly laid layer and several coats may prove necessary. Mixing the glaze with a siccative or drying agent can help. On no account must glaze be painted over underglaze decoration.

Tiles

Tiles are normally glazed on the surface, or on the surface and sides only. They are best coated by skimming them across the surface of the glaze for which process a wide-mouthed bowl is necessary (Figure 11.4).

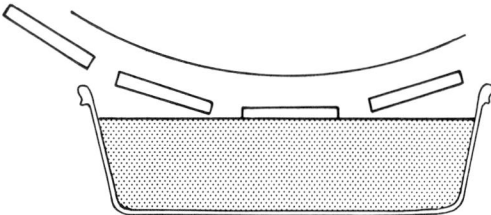

Figure 11.4. Glazing tiles by skimming the surface over glaze held in a bowl

Points to remember

● It is often thought by a beginner that, since glaze becomes molten in the kiln, blobs of dry glaze left after application will flow out. This rarely happens and tidying of the raw glaze before packing in the kiln is very important.

● It is a fallacy to imagine that holding a hard-biscuited pot in the glaze for a longer period of time will increase the thickness of the deposit. In most cases it will have the opposite effect.

● Double-dipping to thicken a layer of glaze or to remedy errors is not always a safe procedure. If it must be done it should be carried out when the initial glaze is still damp.

● Stoneware pots which need to have glaze-free areas such as feet, rims of lids and bases of pillar feet, should have these painted with a resist liquid before glazing. It is better to prevent glaze from adhering than to have to scrape it away later.

● Pots which are not very porous as a result of high temperature biscuiting are best warmed before glazing, since this will bring about quicker drying and consequently, a better coating.

● When glazing the inside of a teapot a small amount of glaze must be poured out through the spout. This should be a quick operation to prevent the grid holes from becoming clogged. It is a good idea to blow down the spout immediately after pouring, whilst the glaze is still mobile, being careful, of course, to avoid direct contact between your mouth and the glaze.

● When pouring glaze over the outside of pots with handles and spouts, it is always advisable to cover the projecting parts first, before covering the remainder.

● Bottles with narrow mouths can be coated on the inside by covering the mouth with the palm of the hand and shaking a little of the glaze around the sides before pouring out the surplus.

● If a bowl has to be given a separate inside and outside colour, the best method is to swill the inside and to plunge-dip the outside.

● The sides of the bucket should be wiped after glazing is completed to prevent powdery flakes dropping down and making resieving necessary.

● Removal of splashes of glaze should be done with a damp cloth. Dry glaze dust must not be brushed into the atmosphere.

146

Storage of glaze

Most glazes can be stored for a considerable time in suitable glass or plastic containers but it must be remembered that fritting is not always a one hundred per cent cure for solubility and it is therefore not good policy to store glazes containing alkaline frits over a long period. All stored glazes must be clearly labelled. Gummed labels stuck onto glass are far from permanent and a 'Dymo'-style label is advised.

12

Kilns and firing

The kiln is the one essential item which every potter must possess in order to bring about the required physical and chemical changes necessary to render the ware serviceable. Kilns can be broadly divided into two types: those in which the heat supplied by flames and hot gases resulting from combustion of raw materials comes directly into contact with the ware and those in which heat is supplied indirectly through a muffle by circulating the warmth between the muffle and the kiln wall. The electric kiln is the only type which does not burn raw fuel, with the result that no gases are created from combustion. Heat can thus be generated by the distribution of heating elements within the muffle itself.

I will not discuss here the home-building of kilns designed to burn wood, coal or oil. This requires considerable technical expertise, and a good working knowledge of the principles of kiln firing should be acquired before the student experiments with designing and building a home kiln. Materials can prove expensive and some form of chimney will be necessary to create sufficient draught. Building such a kiln may, in some districts, raise objections from the Local Authority.

Choosing a kiln

For the amateur potter, the first choice to be made is usually between a kiln heated by electricity and one fired by gas. Generally speaking, the former is considered to be the more suitable for the beginner. It is more easily accommodated, especially in urban areas and in cases where the kiln can only be located within the pottery studio. Since it does not rely on the combustion of raw materials, it requires no specific flue to extract the carbon monoxide and other resultant gases. Installation is therefore a relatively simple matter. Electrically-fired kilns are easy to operate, require little maintenance, and offer the advantage of controlled, even heating. They are available in a wide choice of sizes, making it possible to regulate the size of kiln to the amount of work which will need to be fired. In early electric kilns, the heating elements tended to wear out quickly, but modern 'Kanthal A1' elements give lasting service and are easily obtainable should they need replacement.

The great disadvantage of the electric kiln, however, is that, with a perfectly clean atmosphere, the firing of reduced ware is impossible so you must decide whether this is important or not.

It is possible to buy *gas kilns* which can be fired either by mains or bottled gas. However, they require much more careful siting and the provision of a chimney or flue which is free from down-draughts. Gas kilns are rather more difficult to operate and control with safety than those heated by electricity. Kilns such as those in the 'Gamma' range are excellent and operate quietly, but these are geared more to the commercial potter and are usually too large and expensive for the amateur.

The introduction of the 'Torch' range of portable gas kilns has simplified installation though a flue pipe, with a removable section to allow for top-loading, is still essential. The sizes of these kilns are also more within the range of the amateur, as is their cost. Their maximum temperature is 1300°C and reduction is made possible by covering the top vent at regular periods in accordance with the firing schedule suggested by the makers.

Having made the basic choice between gas and electricity you must now consider temperature range and size. There are many types of electric kilns, both front- and top-loading, from which to choose. The choice must ultimately be an individual one, but it is considered advisable to opt for a kiln which can fire to 1300°C. This gives greater scope by making both earthenware and stoneware firings possible. Even if it is expected to operate for a large proportion of the time around the 1100°C mark, the elements will tend to enjoy a longer life if they are not repeatedly fired to their limits. It is not wise, either, to purchase the very small kilns which are designed specifically for testing. A minimum internal capacity of around 3230 cubic inches (53 litres) is preferable but much will depend on the anticipated amount of ware which it will be necessary to fire at any one time and not least upon the amount of capital available.

Installing an electric kiln

Kilns of reasonable size cannot be merely plugged into a domestic 13-amp socket. They should be installed by a qualified electrician who will advise on the correct connection. It is vital that a good isolation switch is fitted which can be turned off before the kiln door is opened. It will also be necessary to incorporate a control unit and energy regulator into the circuit. This allows for the periods of time during which the switch is closed to be varied and is operated by a manually controlled knob working in conjunction with a scale, calibrated from 0–100, on which settings of 25, 50 and 100 represent 'Low', 'Medium' and 'High' positions. All the elements are on full for varying periods of time, and the lower the setting the longer the 'off' periods. The kiln should be located at least 12 inches (300 mm) from any wall, well away from any draughts. It must rest on a solid and level base to prevent vibration of the elements and so prolong their life.

Installing a gas kiln

A gas kiln should be located in a separate well ventilated room with inlet and outlet grilles and a suitable flue. If it is to be operated on natural gas, the local Gas Board engineer must be contacted to advise on supply, siting and fitting. The kiln itself should be positioned well away from the wall and any inflammable materials, such as curtains, should be removed. It must stand on a concrete floor; wood or other types of floor covering are quite unsuitable.

Kiln temperature

Temperature in a kiln is measured either by the installation of a pyrometer or by placing temperature cones inside it.

The pyrometer is made up of two parts, a thermocouple complete with a compensating cable and adjustable fixing flange, and a standard temperature indicator which is fixed by a suitable mounting bracket, either to the kiln, or to an adjacent wall (Figure 12.1).

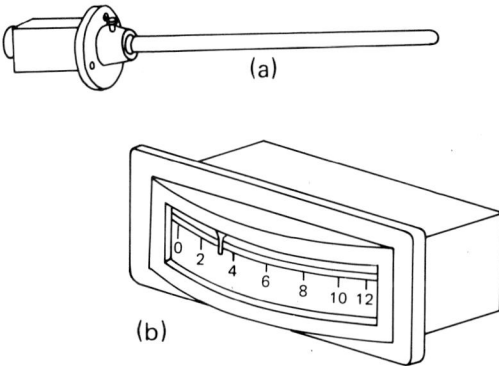

Figure 12.1. The kiln pyrometer. (a) The portion which contains the thermocouple. (b) The standard temperature indicator

The thermocouple is made up of two dissimilar metals, coupled together in a refractory sheath which penetrates into the firing chamber. As the couple is heated, a small electrical current begins to flow which is proportional to the temperature. The current thus generated is measured by a galvanometer and calibrated on the temperature indicator. The usual couple is a platinum/rhodium one which is capable of registering temperatures between 0°C and 1400°C.

Pyrometric cones consist of slender trigonal pyramids of ceramic material chosen to soften and bend (squat, deform) at definite temperatures. They are mounted within the kiln, on a lump of clay or on specially made fire clay cone sockets, at an angle of about 10°–15° from the vertical. The base of each cone is moulded to the correct setting angle. Each cone bears a marker to indicate the temperature at which it will bend. Cones should be set in a position away from the direct influence of an element and in a spot where they are visible from the spy-hole. They are normally used in groups of three, the central cone to represent the required temperature, the

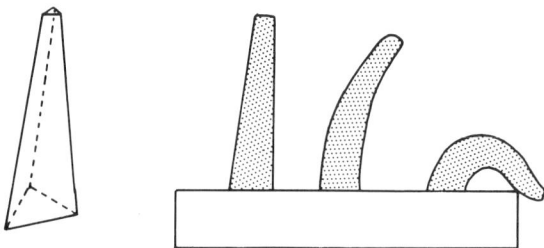

Figure 12.2. Pyrometric cones. (a) General shape. (b) The three cones as they should appear after a satisfactory firing

one on the right to indicate 20°C below it, and the one on the left 20°C above it. The right-hand cone will provide early warning that the correct temperature is being approached and allow heating to be turned off at the precise moment at which the central cone is just half bent over. If the kiln has not been over-fired, the left-hand cone should have remained upright (Figure 12.2).

The pyrometric cone was the invention of Herman Seger, a nineteenth century chemist working at the Royal Porcelain Factory at Charlottesburg, and so the cones are often described as Seger cones. It should be noted that Staffordshire cones bend away from the marked side. It is important to note this when packing a kiln to avoid the risk of their bending onto a nearby glazed pot.

Some suppliers sell cones made by the Orton Ceramic Foundation in America. These are used in a similar fashion, but the series of numbers which they carry do not represent the exact equivalents of the Staffordshire cones, and careful reference to the accompanying table should be made to ensure that the correct sequence of cones is chosen. The Orton cone bends towards its distinguishing mark.

When first getting to know the performance of a new kiln, it is helpful to insert pyrometric cones indicating the required temperature at various points in the firing chamber in addition to the main group, set to be read from the spy-hole. These will provide some indication of the uniformity of temperature maintained within it. Experience is necessary when observing the performance of cones in a luminous kiln as it is sometimes difficult to distinguish the outline. It is helpful, when packing, to make sure that the cones are backed by a pot carrying no similar upright lines, either as part of its general form, or its decoration.

Cones are in many ways more accurate than the pyrometer since they combine a measurement of both temperature and time. The squatting temperatures given in Table 12.1 are based on a regular temperature rise of 240°C per hour, but the slower the rate of temperature rise, the lower the temperature at which the cone will deform. Any table cannot be perfectly accurate for each firing schedule. There is, however, a reasonable tolerance either way and an exact temperature is not usually of great importance. A pyrometer can often be of great help, especially when packing a small kiln, as it is often far from convenient to have to arrange a batt in such a position that the cones resting on it can be observed from the spy-hole, and space can be wasted.

Visible colour changes

In addition to using the accepted methods by which kiln temperature can be judged, it is useful to develop, through

153

Table 12.1 Grades of pyrometric cone

Staffordshire cone number	Approximate squatting temperature	Nearest Orton cone number	Approximate squatting temperature	Kilning ranges
H 018	710°C	018	717°C	
017	730	017	747	
016	750	016	792	Lustres and on-glaze enamels
015	790	015	804	
014	815			
010	900	010	894	
09	920	09	923	
08	940	08	955	
07	960			
06	980	07	984	Stoneware biscuit and
05	1000	06	999	Soft earthenware glaze

Cone	°C	Cone	°C	Description
04	1020			
03	1040			
		05	1046	High earthenware biscuit
02	1060	04	1060	High earthenware glaze
01	1080			
1	1100			
		03	1101	
2	1120	02	1120	
		01	1137	
3	1140			
		1	1154	
4	1160			
5	1180			
		4	1186	
		5	1196	Medium stoneware glaze
6	1200			
		6	1222	
7	1230			
		7	1240	
8	1250			
8A	1260			
		8	1263	High-fired stoneware glaze
9	1280	9	1280	
10	1300			
		10	1305	
		11	1315	
11	1320			

experience, the ability to form a rough estimate of temperature by observing the colours emitted.

At about 500°C, the kiln will appear a dull red. At this time much water is lost and organic matter is burnt out of the clay. As the temperature climbs, the dull red will gradually brighten, and at about 850°C show a bright cherry-red coloured glow. At this stage, dehydration should be complete. With more heat, the red becomes orange-red and then a true orange colour representing a temperature range between 900 and 1000°C. Glazed earthenware pots will begin to take on a wet and shiny appearance as the glaze melts over the surface. Further heat and the orange turns through yellow-orange to yellow. This is a useful indicator that the temperature is between 1050 and 1100°C, the usual temperature for red earthenware biscuit.

Above 1100°C, the yellow fire gradually becomes more and more white as it approaches the melting temperature of stoneware glazes. At around 1250°C the colour inside the kiln has become predominantly white, the phase of high temperature stoneware. A further increase in heat, and the white takes on a bluish haze consistent with temperatures within the 1400–1480°C range, the vitrification point for hard paste porcelains. The colour changes are reversed as the kiln cools down.

Kiln furniture

Shelves in a kiln are usually known as batts and are listed as such in a catalogue. They are heat-conducting and if used with care can have a long life. They should be smaller than both the width and depth of the firing chamber to allow adequate space for the circulation of the hot air within the kiln. They are supported by props which can be in the form of square or tubular pillars of varying heights or of castellated segments which can be notched into each other to provide flexibility in height. The latter are obtainable in two heights, 1 inch (25 mm) and 1½ inch (38 mm), and of the same diameter, and should be used in conjunction with top and bottom base pads which help to distribute the load more evenly (Figure 12.3). It is not a good idea to build up too many of these sections upon one another as the structure can become unstable.

Rectangular blocks are also available, which, since they can be used resting on either face, cater for a variety of heights. Batts are more stable if they rest upon three props arranged

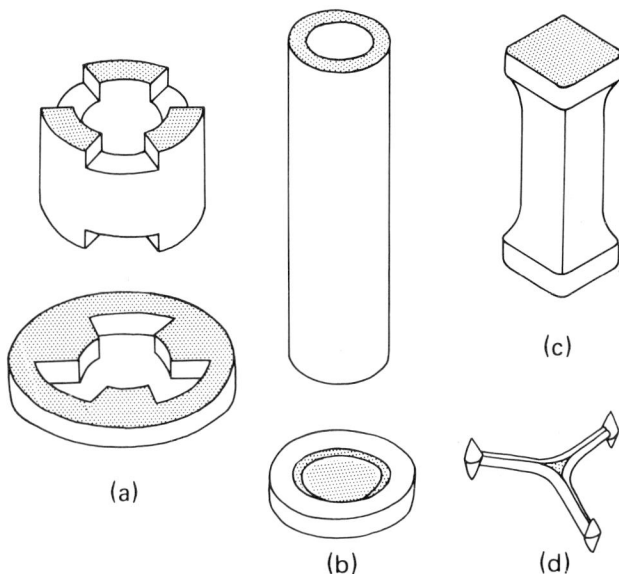

Figure 12.3. Examples of kiln furniture. (a) A castellated prop with base disc. (b) A tubular prop with base support. (c) A square pillar prop. (d) A triangular stilt

in triangular position rather than on four corner props and it is most important that props supporting consecutive batts should be located immediately above one another, that they should be of equal height, and that they are properly seated on the props. Failure to observe these precautions can result in breakages (Figure 12.4).

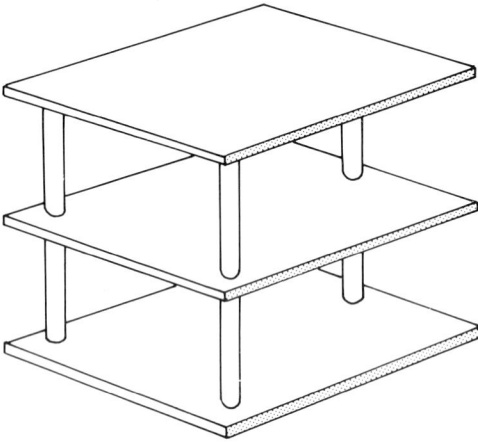

Figure 12.4. Correct positioning of props and kiln shelves

Once a batt has been laid on its props, it is wise to lift it slightly from each in turn, to make sure that it has settled properly. Batts should be stored on edge since flat storage can often lead to breakage, especially if the surface has become uneven due to the deposit of small blobs of glaze. Kits of kiln furniture of correct size are always listed to furnish the many brands of kiln which are on the market.

Packing the kiln

Biscuit kiln
As the packed pieces have no glaze, there is no danger of adhesion, so they can touch one another. The aim is for maximum economy of space commensurate with safety of the pieces and the need to maintain adequate space for circulation within the kiln atmosphere. Smaller shapes may be placed within larger ones, provided that those inside rest over the feet of the container pieces. Cups and bowls may be inverted one over the other provided that the diameters match. A pot with a slightly smaller diameter can become

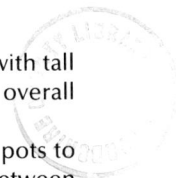

well jammed within the lower supporting piece. Lids with tall knobs can often be inverted on the pot to reduce overall height and so save space (Figure 12.5).

Before packing a kiln, it is a great help to grade the pots to be fired according to their height so that space left between the batts can be reduced to a minimum. A tall pot often has to be incorporated in a batch and can be accommodated more

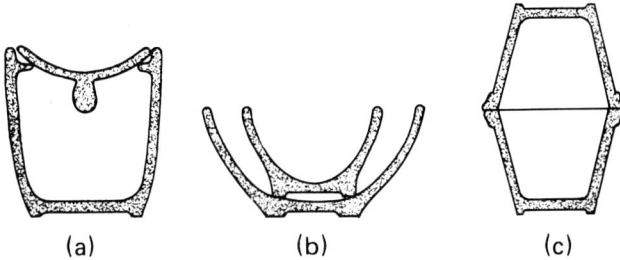

Figure 12.5. Economy in kiln packing. (a) Inverting a lid to save height. (b) Standing one pot inside the contained base of another. (c) Inverting pots of similar diameter one upon the other

easily if a number of small batts are to hand, so that the remaining space can be economically used. Tiles and small mosaic pieces can often be fitted into otherwise empty spaces. Piles of four or five tiles can be built up, if well-supported on each other, by a grid of five or six interlocking stilts.

Earthenware glaze kiln
Earthenware requires as complete a glazing as possible to ensure that the final product is non-porous, so the feet are left covered with a glaze coating.

To prevent the pots from becoming fused to the batt, they are placed on the spurs of refractory stilts which are tapped free when the pots are removed from the kiln. Stilts are graded according to size. Numbers 01, 02, 03 and 04 are good average sizes. If possible, the points of the stilt should rest on the turned foot of the pot (Figure 12.6).

A problem arises with the packing of glazed lids since the diameter of the mouth rarely matches that of a stilt. The best solution is to leave the bottom edge, and a small portion each side of it, free from glaze so that it can rest directly on the batt. This portion will sit within the flange of the pot and so not be visible. For added safety, the edge is often lightly

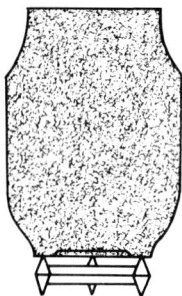

Figure 12.6. Ideally, a stilt should support the foot of a pot

painted with a flint wash. Alternatively, the cleaned lid can be supported on the arms of three stilts. No pots must touch one another or they will fuse together.

Stoneware glaze kiln
Since the clay body becomes more vitreous and plastic when fired at stoneware temperatures, the glazed pots cannot be stilted. This would cause distortion of the base, indeed, the points of the stilt could actually penetrate the softened clay. Pots destined for a stoneware kiln must therefore have the feet and a small adjacent portion of the sides washed, or kept free of glaze and rest directly on the batt.

When packing a glaze kiln of any sort, the pots need careful handling to avoid damage to the raw glaze. This is especially important when Majolica ware, or pots with a pattern sprayed or painted onto the unfired glaze, are being packed. It is also important to wash the fingers between packing pots coated with differently coloured glazes. It is very easy to mar a pot by carrying some glaze from one pot to another. Blue finger-marks on a cream pot, for example, can be disastrous. Before packing, lightly rub over any hair cracks in the layer of glaze with the finger tips. This is especially important in the case of opaque glazes to minimise the danger of crawling. Any excess blobs of glaze should also be smoothed out, especially on the base of earthenware pots which are to be stilted. Any bare patches should be touched up with the appropriate glaze.

Glazed ceramic beads
These are fired by threading them on lines of nichrome wire stretched between two ends of a clay support which has been previously biscuited (Figure 12.7). Care must be taken to

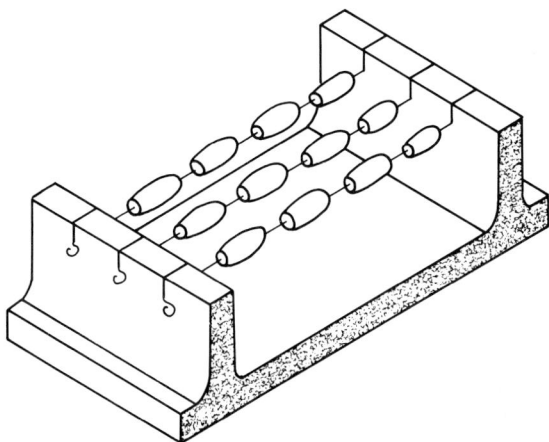

Figure 12.7. A cradle used to support the nickel-chrome wires on which ceramic beads are strung for firing

ensure that the threading holes are glaze-free. Painting the pierced ends with wax can be a help. Too many beads should not be strung onto one line in case the wire sags.

Biscuit and glaze ware should never be fired in the same kiln. Gases from the maturing clay will harm the glaze and glaze volatilising onto biscuit ware can make future glazing difficult.

Enamel kiln

The pieces must be stilted as for earthenware since, although the firing temperature is low, the base glaze will soften slightly.

Firing schedules

It is customary to fire earthenware biscuit hard and to cover it with a glaze maturing at a slightly lower temperature. This technique tends to minimise crazing and makes possible the use of some of the very low-firing glazes (such as chrome red, firing at 875–900°C), which develop striking colours. Stoneware biscuit is usually low-fired to about 1000°C to allow it to be safely handled for decorating and glazing, and then both body and glaze mature at the higher stoneware temperature. Hard paste porcelain, incidentally, is given similar treatment.

The biscuit fire

It has already been noted that pots which appear to be thoroughly dry still contain quite a lot of moisture. Initial firing must proceed very slowly to allow this to be driven off, a period often described as the smoking period. The energy regulator should be set to 'Low heat', mark 25 on the scale, and maintained at this point for at least four hours, the longer you can leave it the safer it will be. If possible it is good policy, to switch to this setting overnight and to increase heat more quickly the following morning. Once the free water has escaped, chemically-combined water will begin to dissociate. Increases in the regulation setting must be gradual until all combined water has been lost. A good simple test is to hold a cold glass above the top ventilator for a second or so and to observe if it mists with condensing steam. The bung should remain withdrawn from the top vent to allow for the escape of steam and other gases from the clay.

When it is certain that all the water has been lost and the kiln shows a red glow, the regulator can safely be advanced to the 'High' setting (100 on the scale) and the top vent closed

162

with the fireclay bung to conserve heat. It then remains to monitor whatever heat-registering device has been installed and to switch off when the correct temperature has been obtained.

The glaze fire
The top bung is left out for the duration of the glaze fire to allow adequate ventilation. This is especially important if the glaze ingredients contain carbonates which will become converted to their corresponding oxides by the loss of carbon dioxide. These must be able to escape to prevent glaze bubbling. Progress to the higher setting can be made quite quickly after an initial hour of warming at a setting of about 35–40 on the regulator. Too rapid a fire can cause pinholing of the glaze.

The enamel fire
This is normally taken to a temperature between 700 and 800°C which can be approached at a fairly quick rate. It is vital not to overfire. The kiln must be well ventilated in the initial warming stage to allow the escape of the colour medium which burns away.

As well as leaving the bung out, it is wise to leave the spy-hole uncovered. Some potters leave the kiln door ajar for the initial burning off phase but this presents a tremendous safety risk and is not to be advised.

Cooling down

After firing is complete, the kiln should be allowed to cool at a natural rate. Much harm can be done to the pots, the elements in an electric kiln and the kiln batts themselves if cold draughts are allowed to enter a very hot kiln by an early opening of the door. Two or three days should be allowed to elapse before opening the kiln. This is especially important for a glaze kiln where there is a danger of the glaze crazing. It is very tempting to see the results of a bake by opening the kiln too early and removing pots whilst still hot, but the temptation must be resisted. Pots which have been stilted will have sharp barbs from the broken off stilt points embedded in the glaze. These can cause severe cuts and should be rubbed down straightaway, with either a file or a carborundum stone.

Assessment of a bake

When a kiln is opened, a careful record should be made of the results for further reference. Much can be learnt from the quality both of the glaze and the biscuit. The colouring of the glazes should be noted against the quantities and materials used in the recipes. In this way, a wealth of valuable information can be assembled concerning optimum strengths of the colouring oxides to be used, the colour response obtainable from varying mixtures of them, the diverse behaviour and colour response of the oxides at differing temperatures, the influence of biscuit tone on transparent colours and the colour changes brought about by glazes built around different fluxes.

Glazed pots which are intended to hold liquids should all be tested to make sure that they are watertight. This is especially important with respect to earthenware. It is not sufficient to make this check merely by filling with water, observing for a few minutes and then re-emptying. The pots should be filled with water and left to stand overnight on a glazed tile or similar glossy surface. Any rings of damp on the tile show that a pot is porous.

A porous pot is usually the result of poor clay and glaze fit and a closer examination of the glaze will probably reveal that the surface is covered with tiny hair cracks. This condition is known as crazing and can usually be cured by adjusting the glaze/clay combination as discussed on page 138.

Bare unglazed patches on the surface of a pot are caused by *crawling*, probably caused by excessive handling of the biscuit ware prior to glazing. Dust and grease can easily be transferred to the pot from dirty hands. Another cause could be the cracking of the raw glaze layer. A pool of glaze may be visible on the batt beneath a pot. This can signify that that particular glaze has received too much fire or that it has been too strongly fluxed. (Some colouring oxides can do this.) The cure is to reduce the flux and to increase the alumina content. On the other hand, a glaze may exhibit all the symptoms of being underfired.

If a glaze is covered with pockmarks it is an indication that it has blistered and the bubbles burst to form tiny craters. The cure is either to fire at a lower temperature or to add more china clay and flint to the glaze recipe in order to raise the maturation temperature. Some glazes, notably those containing manganese dioxide, seem to be prone to bubbling.

Whilst examining the results of the bake, note should be made of any colour changes in a finished pot brought about by its proximity to one coated with a different glaze, some of the ingredients of which have partially volatilised.

It is also worth recording the fate of underglaze colours. This information will provide future guidance concerning the optimum strength in which to apply them.

Finally, defects noted in the pots emerging from a biscuit kiln can often point to errors in making or packing which can then be rectified in the future.

Appendix 1

The theory of glaze building

Glaze materials are all oxides, or become oxides after firing (see Chapter 11). A close examination of active glaze ingredients will show that each will fit into one of three categories:

1. That in which oxygen and the metal combine in a 1:1 ratio.
2. That in which oxygen and the metal combine in a 2:3 ratio and
3. That in which oxygen and the metal combine in a 1:2 ratio.

As observed in the text, the one ingredient defying clear-cut classification is boric oxide (B_2O_3) which seems to have one foot in category 2:3 and one in the category 1:2.

1:1	2:3		1:2
BaO	Al_2O_3		SiO_2
CaO			(TiO_2)
PbO			(SnO_2)
Li_2O			
MgO		B_2O_3	
K_2O			
Na_2O			
SrO			
ZnO			

All the oxides in the first column are bases and behave in a glaze as fluxes, those in the second column are amphoteric and those in column three acidic. Seger labelled the three groups, RO, R_2O_3 and RO_2 respectively, the letter 'R' representing the metal and the proportions in which the active ingredients of a glaze combine are represented under these three headings in what is known as the 'molecular glaze formula'. In order to allow a ready comparison between one formula and another, proportions are always adjusted so that the total of the fluxes adds up to 1.

A glaze is a bi-silicate and must have more than one equivalent part of acid (silica) to one equivalent part of base (flux), but the amount of silica over and above one can vary from one type of glaze to another according to the firing temperature.

The amphoteric (alumina content) is variable within limits but is usually about one tenth to one sixth that of the silica (acid). If B_2O_3 is introduced in conjunction with the silica, it is normally added in the proportion of about one ninth B_2O_3 to eight ninths silica. Thus, a typical earthenware glaze could have the following molecular formula:

RO	R_2O_3	RO_2
1.00	0.3	3.00

and a boro-silicate glaze:

RO	R_2O_3	RO_2
1.00	0.4	4.00
	0.45	B_2O_3

To build a glaze from the molecular formula, it is necessary to select those materials which provide the required active ingredients in the correct given proportion. It is possible to create several recipes, all of which satisfy the proportions called for, the active ingredients being present in a variety of different minerals, chemicals or frits, for example K_2O can be introduced in the form of potash feldspar or as Cornish stone, lithium in the form of petalite or as lithium carbonate. The method by which a glaze recipe is built up from the given molecular formula is best illustrated by means of a specific example.

Suppose that a batch of glaze is to be made up, having the following structure:

	RO Flux	R_2O_3 Alumina	RO_2 Silica
K_2O	0.296	0.519	3.69
CaO	0.390		
BaO	0.313		

The K_2O can be introduced as potash feldspar, the CaO as whiting, the BaO as barium carbonate, the alumina as china clay and the silica as flint. But potash feldspar contains also one part of alumina and six parts of silica and so will supply some of the required amount of these ingredients. Similarly, china clay contains two parts of silica as well as the alumina. It is therefore necessary to keep a tally of the various materials being introduced in the form of a table thus:

Ingredient	K_2O	CaO	BaO	Al_2O_3	SiO_2
Potash feldspar $(K_2O.Al_2O_3.6SiO_2)$	0.296			0.296	(6×0.296) $= 1.776$
Whiting $(CaCO_3)$		0.390			
Barium carbonate $(BaCO_3)$			0.313		
China clay $(Al_2O_3\ 2SiO_2)$				$(0.519 - 0.296)$ $= 0.223$	(2×0.223) $= 0.446$
Flint (SiO_2)					$3.69 - (1.776 + 0.446)$ $= 1.468$
Totals	0.296	0.390	0.313	0.519	3.69

The following *proportion* of ingredients will therefore satisfy the glaze formula:

Potash feldspar	0.296
Whiting	0.390
Barium carbonate	0.313
China clay	0.233
Flint	1.468

Actual *amounts* required in the glaze batch are determined by multiplying in each case by the molecular weight of the ingredient – thus:

Ingredient	Proportion	× Molecular weight	= Quantity
Potash feldspar	0.296	556	164.457
Whiting	0.390	100	39.000
Barium carbonate	0.313	197.36	61.773
China clay	0.233	258	57.534
Flint	1.468	60.06	88.168
		Total	410.932

In practice, it is more convenient to quote the recipe in percentage form. This can be achieved by dividing the quantity of each ingredient by their sum total, and multiplying by 100. For example:

$$\text{Potash feldspar} \quad \frac{164.457 \times 100}{410.932} = 40.02$$

and so the percentage glaze recipe could read:

Potash feldspar	40.02
Whiting	9.49
Barium carbonate	15.00
China clay	14.00
Flint	21.46

which can be weighed out in any weight unit.

Adjustment of a glaze recipe can be more easily effected if the molecular glaze formula is known. This can be determined from a given recipe by working backwards and is best illustrated by taking the same example which has just been worked out.

The first step is to divide each of the amounts in the recipe by the appropriate molecular weight:

Ingredient	Amount	÷	Molecular weight	=	Proportional parts
Potash feldspar	40.02		556		0.072
Whiting	9.49		100		0.095
Barium carbonate	15.00		197.36		0.076
China clay	14.00		258		0.054
Flint	21.46		60.06		0.357

From which the following analysis can be made, remembering, as before, that the feldspar and the china clay contain more than one substance.

Ingredient	Fluxes			Alumina	Silica
	K_2O	CaO	BaO	Al_2O_3	SiO_2
Potash feldspar	0.072			0.072	0.432
					(6×0.072)
Whiting		0.095			
Barium carbonate			0.76		
China clay				0.054	0.108
					(2×0.054)
Flint					0.357
	0.072	0.095	0.76	0.519	0.897

The molecular glaze formula can therefore be written as:

	RO	R_2O_3	RO_2
K_2O	0.072		
CaO	0.095	0.519	0.897
BaO	0.076		
Total	0.243		

As mentioned earlier, the proportions are always presented in a form in which the fluxes add up to 1. The final form, therefore, can be achieved by dividing each by the sum total of the fluxes.

Thus; $0.072 \div 0.243 = 0.296$
$0.095 \div 0.243 = 0.390$
$0.076 \div 0.243 = 0.313$
$0.126 \div 0.243 = 0.519$
$0.897 \div 0.243 = 3.690$

	RO	R_2O_3	RO_2
K_2O	0.296		
CaO	0.390	0.519	3.690
BaO	0.313		
Total	1.000		

Which is that quoted at the outset.

Appendix 2

Glaze recipes

Suggested schedule for beginners using stock glazes

Earthenware. Red earthenware body biscuit fired to 1120°C and clear glazed with either Podmore glaze P.2105 or P.2106 or opaque glazed with Podmore glaze P.2114; all fired to 1100°C
Stoneware. Buff prepared stoneware body biscuit fired to 1060°C and clear glazed with Podmore glaze P.2108 or opaque glazed with Podmore glaze P.2120; both fired to 1260°C.

Glaze recipes

The student is advised to prepare a small quantity of any chosen recipe (adding colourants if required) and test fire it before preparing a quantity batch.

Earthenware
The following glazes (1–8) are all transparent and bright and can be coloured as required and/or opacified.

1.	Lead bisilicate	52.5	T. 1060–1080°C
	Soda feldspar	20.4	
	Colemanite	13.8	
	China clay	7.5	
	Flint	5.0	
	Zirconium oxide	0.9	

2. Lead bisilicate   52.8   T. 1060–1080°C
    Soda feldspar   13.0
    Podmore frit P2244   12.3
    Strontium carbonate   5.1
    Zirconium oxide   0.6
    China clay   9.9
    Flint   6.1

3. Lead bisilicate   64.8   T. 1080–1100°C
    Fulham alkaline frit F.P.3003   8.7
    Zinc oxide   5.5
    Whiting   2.3
    China clay   6.3
    Potash feldspar   12.5

4. Fulham borax frit F.P.3002   45.78   T. 1100°C
    Potash feldspar   40.30
    Whiting   11.05

5. Lead bisilicate   81.4   T. 1080–1100°C
    Whiting   6.8
    China clay   10.7
    Flint   1.0

With the addition of 3 per cent cobalt oxide, 2 per cent red oxide
of iron and 2 per cent manganese dioxide this makes a good
black.

6. Lead bisilicate   83.0   T. 1080–1100°C
    Cornish stone   12.2
    Flint   4.8

With the addition of 3 per cent red oxide of iron, this makes an
excellent clear amber glaze which is very suitable for slipwares.
2.5 per cent red oxide of iron and 0.6 per cent black copper oxide
gives a celadon.

7. Lead bisilicate   24.3   1060–1080°C
    Podmore P.2246 frit   38.8
    Cornish stone   29.1
    China clay   7.8

8. Potash feldspar   44   T. 1060–1080°C
   Colemanite   30
   Zinc oxide   5
   Barium carbonate   6
   China clay   4
   Flint   10

9. Lead bisilicate   87.2   T. 1080–1100°C
   Potash feldspar   7.4
   China clay   3.5
   Rutile   1.9
A bright clear amber glaze with brown speckle.

10. Lead bisilicate   51.9   T. 1080–1100°C
    Whiting   4.4
    Cornish stone   18.8
    Potash feldspar   10.4
    China clay   4.8
    Flint   9.8
    Black copper oxide   4.0
A good semi-opaque green glaze.

11. Podmore P.2244 frit   25.2   T. 1080–1100°C
    Potash feldspar   42.3
    Talc   7.0
    Barium carbonate   9.0
    Zinc oxide   2.5
    China clay   4.7
    Flint   9.3
A semi-transparent glaze.

12. Lead bisilicate   59.7   T. 1080–1100°C
    Whiting   5.2
    Zinc oxide   9.9
    China clay   25.2
This is a matt glaze built up on the principles quoted on page 132.

13. Podmore P.2246 borax frit 37.5   T. 1080–1100°C
    Lead bisilicate   37.0
    Cornish stone   16.0
    Red oxide of iron   6.0
    Black copper oxide   1.0
    Iron chromate   3.0
A clear, bright, black glaze.

Stoneware

Comments refer to firing in an electric (oxidising) kiln.

1. Lithium carbonate   6.9   T. 1230–1260°C
   Dolomite   9.5
   Colemanite   13.1
   China clay   30.5
   Flint   40.1

A bright, clear glaze.

2. Petalite   33   T. 1220–1230°C
   Whiting   9.3
   Colemanite   30.0
   Ball clay   17.6
   Flint   10.0

A clear transparent glaze.

3. Potash feldspar   49.7   T. 1300°C
   Whiting   20.7
   China clay   29.6

A matt glaze

4. Potash feldspar   40.2   T. 1280-1300°C
   Whiting   9.5
   Barium carbonate   15.0
   China clay   14.0
   Flint   21.4

An opaque semi-matt glaze.

5. Potash feldspar   36.5   T. 1260°C
   Dolomite   23.4
   Whiting   5.3
   Zinc oxide   3.4
   China clay   15.9
   Flint   15.5

A semi-opaque matt glaze.

6. Wood ash   60   T. 1260°C
   Potash feldspar   40
   Flint   8

Variable with type of ash used.

7.	Cornish stone	37.8	T.1260°C
	Talc	9.6	
	Whiting	19.7	
	Ball clay	19.0	
	Flint	14.1	

A semi-clear glaze.

Appendix 3

Bibliography

Birks, Tony. 1980. *Basic Pottery*. A. H. and W. Reed, Alpha Books, Sherborne, Dorset.

Birks, Tony. 1982. *The New Potter's Companion*. Wm. Collins, Sons and Co. Ltd., London.

Colson, Frank A. 1976. *Kiln Building with Space-Age Materials*. Van Nostrand Reinhold Co. New York.

Cooper, Emmanuel. 1980. *The Potter's Book of Glaze Recipes*. B. T. Batsford Ltd., London.

Cowley, David, 1978. *Moulded and Slipcast Pottery and Ceramics*. B. T. Batsford Ltd., London.

Gregory, Ian. 1977. *Kiln Building*. Pitman. London.

Hamer, Frank and Hamer, Janet. 1977. *Clays*. Pitman. London.

Hamilton, David. 1982. *Manual of Stoneware and Porcelain*. Thames and Hudson, London.

Jorgensen, Gunhild, 1981. *The Technique of China Painting*. Van Nostrand Reinhold Co. Ltd., London.

Pollex, John. 1976. *Slipware*. Pitman, London.

Priolo, Joan B., and Priolo, Antony. 1980. *Ceramics by Coil and Slab*. Stirling Publishing Co., U.S.A.

Rhodes, Daniel. 1969. *Kilns: Design, Construction and Operation*. Pitman, London.

Rhodes, Daniel. 1973. *Clay and Glazes for the Potter*. Pitman, London.

Sandeman, Alison. 1978. *Working with Porcelain*. Pitman, London.

Shafer, Thomas. 1976. *Pottery Decoration*. Pitman, London.

Southwell, Sheila. 1980. *Painting China and Porcelain*. Blandford Press Ltd., Poole.

Appendix 4

Suppliers

Great Britain

Potterycrafts Ltd. Shelton, Stoke-on-Trent, Staffordshire, ST1 4PQ. This company now incorporates the businesses of Podmore and Sons Ltd., Podmore Ceramics Ltd., Wengers, and Harrison Mayer. They also have showrooms and sales offices in London at 105 Minet Road, SW9 7UH and 75 Silver Street, N18 1RP.

The Fulham Pottery Ltd., Burlington House, 184 New Kings Road, London, SW6 4PB. Also have a Potter's Shop at 42 Morley Road, Tonbridge, Kent.

Messrs. Potclays, Brickkiln Lane, Etruria, Stoke-on-Trent, ST4 7BD.

The Moira Pottery Co. Ltd., Moira, Leicestershire.

Cromartie Kilns Ltd., Park Hall Road, Longton, Stoke-on-Trent. Kiln specialists but also general ceramic suppliers.

Messrs. Kasenit Ltd., Denbigh Road, Bletchley, Milton Keynes, Buckinghamshire, MK1 1EQ. Gas Kilns.

USA

General suppliers

Kickwheel Pottery Supply, 1428 Mayson Street, N.E. Atlanta, Georgia 30324.

Miami Clay Co. Inc., 4446 S.W. 74th Avenue, Miami, Florida 33155.

American Art Clay Co. Inc., 4717 West Sixteenth Street, Indianapolis, Indiana 46222.

Westwood Ceramic Supply Co., 14400 Lomitas Avenue, Dept. BO 67, City of Industry, California 91746.

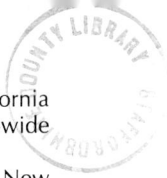

Robert Brent Corporation, P.O. Box 968, Healdsburg, California 95448. (From whom a comprehensive list of world-wide distributors can be obtained).

Byrne Ceramic Supply Co. Inc., 95 Bartley Road, Flanders, New Jersey 07836.

Santa Fe Clay Co., 540 So. Guadelupe, Santa Fe, New Mexico 87501.

Marjon Ceramics Inc., 3434 West Earll Drive, Phoenix, Arizona 85017 and at 426 West Alturas, Tucson, Arizona 85705.

Armadillo Clay & Supplies, 3307 East 4th Street, Austin, Texas 78702.

Ceramic Supply of New York & North Jersey, 534 La Guardia Place, New York, New York.

Clays

Columbus Clay Co., 1331 Edgehill Road, Columbus, Ohio 43212.

Industrial Minerals Co., 7268 Frasinetti Road, Florin, California 95828. (From whom a complete list of distributors can be obtained.)

Standard Ceramic Supply Co., P.O. Box 4435, Pittsburgh, Pennsylvania 15205.

Trinity Ceramic Supply Inc., 9016, Diplomacy Row, Dallas, Texas 75247.

Electric kilns

Ceramic Fiber Fabrication Inc., 878 South Rose Place, Anaheim, California 92805.

Paragon Industries, Dept. CM-13, Box 10133, Dallas, Texas 75207.

Skutt Ceramic Products, 2618 S.E. Steele Street, Portland, Oregon 97202.

Crusader Ceramic Equipment, 4717 W. 16th Street, Indianapolis, Indiana 46222.

Gas kilns

Olympic Kilns, 6301 Button Gwinnett Drive, Atlanta, Georgia 30340.

A.D. Alpine Inc., Dept. B, 3051 Fujita Street, Torance, California 90505.

Contemporary Kiln Inc., P.O. Box 573, Novato, California 94948 (Also electric kilns.)

Bailey Pottery Equipment Corp., C.P.O. 1577, Kingston, New York 12401. (Also electric kilns.)

Potter's wheels

Soldner Pottery Equipment Inc., P.O. Box 428, Silt, Colorado 81652.

Creative Industries, 5366 Jackson Drive, La Mesa, California 92041.

Canada

Plainsman Clays Ltd., Box 1266, Medicine Hat, Alberta T1A 7M9.

Alberta Ceramic Supplies Ltd., 11565–149th Street, Edmonton, Alberta.

Island Ceramic Supplies, Island Highway, Nanaimo, British Columbia.

The Ceramic Greenhouse Ltd., 31 Trottier Bay, Winnipeg, Manitoba.

Ceramic Arts & Crafts Supply, 2280 Industrial Street, Burlington, Ontario.

Harris Ceramic Supplies (Quebec) Inc., 800 Jean Brillon, La Salle, Quebec.

M & G Ceramics Ltd., 4229 Dewdney Avenue, Regina, Saskatchewan.

Australia

Aldrax Industries Pty. Ltd., Cnr. South & Euston Street, Rydalmere, Sydney, New South Wales.

Ceramic Supply Center, Unit 2, 429 Creek Road, Mount Gravatt, Brisbane, Queensland.

Duncan Ceramic Products (Australia), 7 Wanda Avenue, Findon, South Australia.

Ceramicraft of Western Australia, 28 Colray Street, Osborne Park, West Australia.

New Zealand

Smith & Smith Ltd., 213–215 Tuan Street, Christchurch, New Zealand.

Appendix 5

Glossary

Batt 1. A slab of plaster or fired clay. 2. A refractory kiln shelf.

Bentonite A clay possessing above-average plasticity.

Biscuit ware Sometimes known as bisque – pottery which has been fired once but not glazed.

Body A blend of clays prepared for a specific type of ware.

Bone china A form of English porcelain containing a large proportion of calcined bone.

Chamfer The surface made by cutting away an edge at 45° angle.

Cottle An improvised wall of linoleum or similar material erected around a clay shape during casting to retain the liquid plaster.

Deflocculation The breaking down of natural electrical bonds in a clay structure to aid the preparation of casting slip.

Development A shape marked out on a flat surface which can be bent up to form a three-dimensional object.

Fettle line The seam line on a pot resulting from the meeting of two parts of a plaster mould.

Frit A melted mixture of silica and flux to render the latter insoluble.

Former Any solid over which a pliable material may be shaped.

Green ware Pottery which has not yet been fired.

Grog Reground biscuit.

Lawn A phosphor-bronze pottery sieve.

Luting Joining and modelling together pieces of leather-hard clay with the aid of slip.

Mitre A joint meeting at a 45° angle.

Natch hole Sometimes known as a joggle. Sockets cut into one part of a plaster mould prior to pouring an adjacent portion to ensure accurate registration.

Paddle A piece of wood shaped in the form of a small paddle and used in the shaping of hand-built pots.

Pyrometer A device for measuring high temperatures in a kiln.

Refractory A material which can resist a high temperature.

Resist agent Any substance which may be used to mask a surface and so prevent its being coated with a general slip, colour or glaze.

Rutile Crude oxide of titanium.

Slip Clay mixed with water to a liquid consistency.

Sprig A unit of low relief ornament produced in a small plaster mould.

Vellum glaze A semi-matt glaze which has a satin-like appearance.

Vitreous Glass-like.

Vitrification The formation of glass-like material in a clay body.

Volatilise To turn into a vapour.

Weathering Exposing clay over a long period after digging to the elements.

Wooden slat A short length of wood cut and prepared to a predetermined thickness.

Index